Test Expert

Speaking Practice for **CELPIP**®

Christien Lee

Thanks to M and K (and T as well) for letting me have the time to write this. I love you all.

TABLE OF CONTENTS

HOW to USE THIS BOOK

This book is designed to help you improve your ability to deliver effective responses to the eight speaking tasks in the CELPIP Test. It is not designed to be a complete guide to speaking in English. Instead, it offers advice that is specific to the tasks you will see in the speaking section of CELPIP. If you study this guide carefully and practice giving responses based on the expert responses in this guide, you will become a more effective speaker and probably raise your test score.

Key Features

This book has many valuable features designed to help you give more effective responses to the kinds of speaking questions you will see in the CELPIP Test:

- Detailed introductions to each speaking task, including images that show how the screen will look.

- Step-by-step guides that explain how to deliver effective responses to each speaking task.

- 48 speaking topics in total (six for each task) that are designed to be similar to the tasks in the real test.

- 40 model responses by a test expert that are likely to score 11 or 12, including some that include a detailed analysis and explanation.

- 40 practice and challenge activities to help you understand how to produce great responses.

- Explanations of common problems that test-takers experience together with practical solutions to avoid making those mistakes.

- Useful lists of natural words and phrases that you can use in your own responses to sound like a native speaker of English.

Suggested Approach

You can use this book in any way that will benefit you, but following these steps is recommended:

STEP 1   Read the introduction to CELPIP, the introduction to the Speaking test, and the explanation of how the speaking test is scored on pages 8 to 10.

STEP 2   Read the introductory information about Speaking Task 1. The introductory information includes:

- a detailed overview and introduction to the task on page 11

- information about how to organize your response on page 14

- a step-by-step guide to responding to Task 1 questions on page 14

- information about common mistakes and list of useful phrases on page 16

STEP 3   Study the sample response to a Task 1 question and the analysis of it on page 17. Make sure you understand why the sample response is a good one. You may wish to practice saying the sample response a number of times until you can say it naturally and fluently in the allowed time.

STEP 4   Do practice exercises 1.1, 1.2, and 1.3 on pages 18 to 20. After completing each exercise, check your answers at the back of the book. Then practice saying each response repeatedly until you can say it naturally and fluently in the allowed time.

STEP 5   Do practice 1. 4 on page 21. After completing your response, compare it with the test expert's suggested response at the back of the book and find ways to improve your answer. Then practice saying your response until you can say it naturally and fluently in the allowed time.

STEP 6   Do practice 1.5 on page 21 under test conditions. Record your response, if possible, and listen to it critically. Think about how you could improve your response.

STEP 7   Repeat steps 2 to 6 for Task 2, Task 3, Task 4, Task 5, Task 6, Task 7, and Task 8.

STEP 8   After you have reviewed all of the information in this book, continue practicing speaking daily. There are many ways you can keep practicing, such as

- say at least five of the test expert's model responses in this book each day

- come up with new responses for practice 4 and practice 5 for each speaking task

- come up with responses to CELPIP-style speaking questions in other study books

  (see Appendix 1 on page 116 for advice about finding other useful study materials)

Authentic Speaking Practice

Note that when you deliver speaking responses under test conditions in step 6, you may want to use the free CELPIP sample test available from Paragon Testing Enterprises. Doing this will give you very authentic speaking practice that is essentially the same as the real test experience. To use the free test in this way, follow these steps:

- Visit https://secure.paragontesting.ca/InstructionalProducts/ and click on the orange button marked "Start Sample Test."

- Choose either "Free Online Sample Test – G" or "Free Online Sample Test – LS" from the drop-down menu and then click "OK."

- Click the orange button marked "Start" and then choose "Speaking" from the drop-down menu.

- When the speaking directions appear, click "Next" until the task you want to practice appears on the screen. For example, if you wanted to practice Speaking Task 1, you would need to click "Next" twice.

- Use the times and information on screen to tell you how much preparation time and recording time remain, but respond to the questions in this book instead of the questions on screen.

After you have recorded your responses, you may wish to ask a teacher (or someone else whose judgement you trust) to give feedback on them. Then listen to them yourself and find at least five things to improve.

Note that if you use this free sample test to get authentic practice, your responses will not be recorded. If you want to record then, you will need to use your computer, tablet, phone, or other device. (If you are not sure how to do this, search the Internet or ask somebody who is good with technology for help.)

Hear the Suggested Responses

All of the model responses in this book have been recorded by the author. You can listen to him saying them if you subscribe to the "Test Expert" YouTube channel.

This channel will also have videos giving advice about other parts of CELPIP. You can find this channel by searching for "test expert CELPIP" on YouTube. (If you have trouble finding the channel, visit this site: http://tinyurl.com/TestExpert.)

Listening to the suggested responses and trying to copy the rhythm, intonation, and pronunciation that you hear may help you sound more natural when you speak.

About the Author

The author, Christien Lee, was born in the UK, but has lived in Canada since 2002. He started teaching in 1992. Since 1997 he has specialized in helping people pass English language tests such as CELPIP, IELTS, TOEFL IBT, TOEIC, PTE Academic, MELAB, as well as Cambridge tests like KET, PET, FCE, and CAE.

In addition to his work as a language teacher, he has been a teacher-trainer, a curriculum developer, a materials writer, a language training consultant, an e-learning developer, a programmer, and an author.

He has written the following books:

- A TOEFL iBT textbook published by Oxford University Press

- A MELAB study guide published by Cambridge Michigan Language Assessments

- An academic skills book based on TED Talks published by Cengage / National Geographic Learning

- An LPI Writing guide published by Paragon Testing Enterprises
  (this is the organization that develops and administers the CELPIP Test)

Writing Guide

The same author has also written a book similar to this one that gives you practice for the writing section of the CELPIP-General Test. The writing guide includes a detailed step-by-step guide and introduction to each writing task, over 20 model responses for each task, numerous practice and challenge activities, and a list of useful words and phrases.

The guide to writing should be available at the same place where you bought this guide to speaking.

INTRODUCTION TO CELPIP®

CELPIP is a computer-based English language proficiency test. The name stands for Canadian English Language Proficiency Index Program. There are three versions of the test: CELPIP-General (or CELPIP-G), which tests reading, listening, speaking, and writing; CELPIP-LS, which tests listening and speaking only; and CELPIP-Academic. **This book is designed to help people taking either CELPIP-G or CELPIP-LS.**

There are four sections in CELPIP-G, but CELPIP-LS includes only the listening and speaking sections:

	Section	Description	Time
1	Listening	The listening section has six scored parts and one unscored part. You will listen to two conversations between two people, listen to one person interviewing another person, watch a video that shows two or three people talking, and listen to two talks or reports.	~40 minutes
2	Reading	The reading section has four scored parts and one unscored part. You will read several letters, emails, and short texts. You will also have to read information about diagrams or photographs.	60 minutes
3	Writing	The writing section has two scored tasks. It does not have any unscored tasks. You will write one email based on information that is given to you. You will also write a response to a survey question.	53 minutes
4	Speaking	The speaking section has one unscored practice task and eight scored tasks. The tasks include things like expressing your opinion about a topic, giving advice to somebody, describing a personal experience, and describing what you can see in a picture.	~20 minutes

Both CELPIP-G and CELPIP-LS are computerized tests. Every part of the test will take place on a computer, including the speaking and writing sections. If you are not comfortable using a computer, practice as much as possible before your test.

Introduction to the Speaking Test

Speaking is the final part of CELPIP. At the start of the speaking test, you will see specific instructions about how to answer the speaking test. The instructions will look similar to this:

CELPIP-General – Speaking Test

> **ⓘ Speaking Test Instructions**
>
> - There are 9 tasks in this test: one practice task and eight scored tasks.
> - The instructions and questions are in writing. You will not hear them.
> - For each task, there are two timed sections: Preparation Time and Recording Time. You will be able to see these times in the top right corner of the screen.
> - The test will record your answers automatically.
> - If you do not finish a task in the time provided, the screen will move to the next task. You cannot go back to the previous task.

The speaking section lasts approximately 20 minutes and has one unscored practice task and eight scored tasks. These tasks are intended to be similar to the kinds of speaking tasks that people do in daily life:

Task	Question Type	Preparation Time	Speaking Time
–	Practice question (unscored)	30 seconds	60 seconds
1	Giving advice	30 seconds	90 seconds
2	Talking about a personal experience	30 seconds	60 seconds
3	Describing a scene	30 seconds	60 seconds
4	Making predictions	30 seconds	60 seconds
5	Comparing (Part 1)	60 seconds	–
	Comparing and Persuading (Part 2)	30 seconds	60 seconds
6	Dealing with a difficult situation	60 seconds	60 seconds
7	Expressing opinions	30 seconds	90 seconds
8	Describing an unusual situation	30 seconds	60 seconds

How the Speaking Test is Scored

Two specially-trained raters will assess your responses, with each rater assessing four responses. The raters will use four criteria when judging your responses:

Description and Explanation of Scoring Criteria

1   Coherence / Meaning

How clear your ideas are and how well your ideas work together

- Have you explained your ideas clearly?

- Have you organized your response in a way that makes it easy for the rater to follow your ideas?

- Have you shown the ability to express information precisely and with deep meaning?

2   Lexical Range

How accurately and naturally you use vocabulary

- Does your response have a sufficient range of vocabulary to complete the task well?

- Have you shown the ability to use natural words and phrases to express ideas accurately?

3   Listenability / Comprehensibility

How fluent your speaking is and how easy it is to understand

- Are grammar, word use, or pronunciation errors likely to confuse the rater?

- Have you used a variety of different sentence types, effectively and naturally?

- Does your response have good rhythm and intonation, and do you use pauses naturally?

4   Task Fulfillment

How well your response addresses the task

- Does your response answer every part of the task effectively?

- Is your response long enough and does it include relevant information?

- Is the tone of your response appropriate, or is it too formal or informal?

The rater will assign you a score out of 12 for each criterion. Your final mark from each rater will be the average of the scores for each criterion. Your final score for the speaking test will be the average of the scores you received from the two raters.

Note that the raters will *not* listen to your responses as you say them. They will listen to your recorded responses a short time after you have taken the test.

TIPS FOR CELPIP®

Following these strategies and study tips may help you achieve a better score in the speaking section of CELPIP.

Study Tip 1 – Practice All the Time

Every time you speak in English, you have an opportunity to improve the skills you will need for CELPIP. For example, if a friend has a problem, you could give him or her advice in the same way you would respond to a Task 1 question in CELPIP. Or if your boss asks for your opinion about something, you could answer her question in the same way you would respond to a Task 7 question in CELPIP. Or if somebody wants to know what might happen later, you could answer using the same kind of language you would use in a response to a Task 4 question in CELPIP. In addition, you can give yourself mini speaking challenges whenever you have a few spare minutes. For example, if you are taking a bus, you could practice talking about a personal experience in your mind. As a simple rule, the more often you practice, the more likely you are to improve.

Study Tip 2 – Be Accurate and Natural Rather Than Advanced

The scoring criteria for CELPIP do NOT say your speaking must be advanced. To score well, it is often better to use a variety of relatively simple English that is accurate and natural rather than trying to use advanced language, but using it in incorrect or unnatural ways. This is especially true because a response that uses advanced language but which has mistakes is more likely to confuse the raters, which can have a significant effect on your overall score.

Study Tip 3 – Speak about Familiar Topics

When deciding which ideas to speak about, always try to choose something that is familiar to you and that you have previously spoken (or written) about in English. Talking about unfamiliar topics or ideas will probably cause you to make more mistakes and speak less fluently, both of which will affect your score.

Study Tip 4 – Listen Actively to Other Speakers

When you listen to other people speaking English, listen actively and focus not just on what they say, but also on how they say it. If you hear a speaker say something very clearly or well, make a note of what you heard and try using the same expressions or same grammar patterns when you speak English. (Copying other people is the way we all learn our first language, and it can still be a useful strategy for becoming better at speaking for tests like CELPIP. This is why you can hear all of the responses in this book on the "Test Expert" YouTube channel.)

SPEAKING TASK 1

Task 1 – Introduction

After the practice task, you will see Task 1, which is the first scored task. Task 1 questions ask you to give advice to someone about how to deal with a common or familiar situation. **You will have 30 seconds in which to prepare your response, and 90 seconds in which to deliver your response.**

In some cases, the topic will give you a choice between two options; in other cases, you will have to give advice about just one situation.

Your focus in Task 1 should be to give clear, direct advice and to support that advice with detailed, logical reasons and/or examples. As with every speaking task, there is no right answer or preferred response.

During the **preparation time** for Task 1, the computer screen will look something like this:

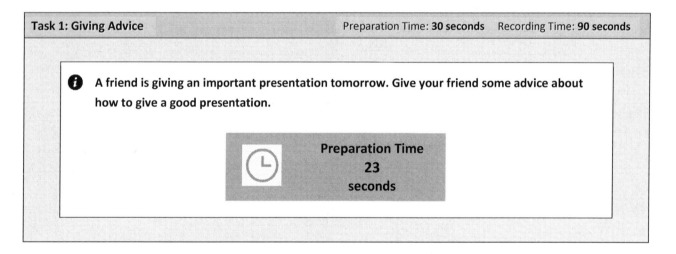

Task 1: Giving Advice	Preparation Time: **30 seconds** Recording Time: **90 seconds**

ⓘ A friend is giving an important presentation tomorrow. Give your friend some advice about how to give a good presentation.

Preparation Time
23
seconds

At the top of the screen, you will see the title bar, which shows the speaking task you are currently doing, how much time you have to prepare, and how much time you have in which to speak.

In the middle of the screen, you will see the topic. Below the topic, you will see an icon of a clock and a timer. The timer will count down until there is no more preparation time remaining.

After the preparation time has finished, the computer will automatically go on to the recording screen, which will look similar to this:

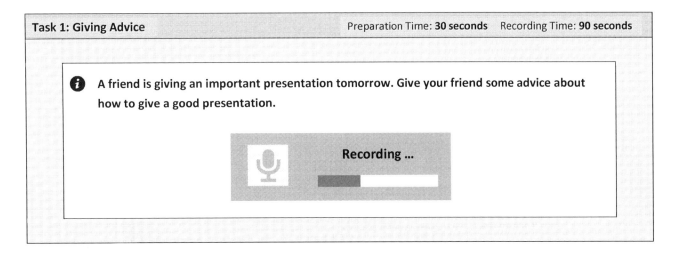

In the middle of the screen you will see an icon of a microphone as well as a bar showing the amount of time remaining in which to record your response. As soon as you see this screen, you should begin speaking. The computer will automatically record what you say. (You do not need to click anything to start recording.)

不用点~

After the recording time is up, the computer will stop recording automatically. The screen will change and look similar to this:

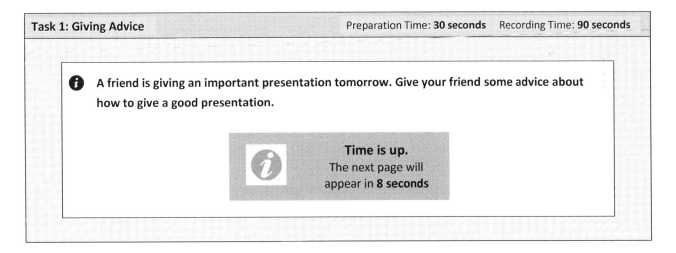

When the computer stops recording, it will automatically save your response. You do not need to click anything to save the response. After a few seconds, the computer will automatically go on to Task 2.

Task 1 – How to Organize Your Response

Depending on the topic you get, there are three typical ways to organize your response to Task 1 questions. As you can see, the introduction and conclusion are the same for all three types of topic.

Some Task 1 topics ask you to advise somebody about the better of two choices. In such cases, it is a good idea to organize your response like this:

type 1
直接给的建议

	Your friend might take a vacation in Canada or in the USA. What advice do you have for her?

↓ 刀两优点，两缺点.

Introduction	• Greet the other person and introduce what you are going to say
Body of Speech	• Discuss at least two advantages of the choice you recommend • Discuss at least two disadvantages of the choice you do *not* recommend
Conclusion	• Add a concluding statement and express a wish or hope about the situation

Some Task 1 topics ask you to discuss both the advantages and disadvantages of doing something, or what somebody should and should not do. In such cases, it is a good idea to organize your response like this:

type 2
这个未定的
adv and disad

	Your friend might quit his job. Advise him on the advantages and disadvantages of doing this.

↓

Introduction	• Greet the other person and introduce what you are going to say
Body of Speech	• Discuss at least two advantages of the choice you recommend • Discuss at least two disadvantages of the choice you recommend
Conclusion	• Add a concluding statement and express a wish or hope about the situation

And some Task 1 topics ask you to give advice to somebody about how to do something well or how to deal with a situation. In such cases, you should probably organize your response like this:

type 3:
怎样做好

	A friend is giving a presentation tomorrow. Advise her how to give a good presentation.

↓

Introduction	• Greet the other person and introduce what you are going to say
Body of Speech	• Give at least two pieces of advice to the person 给他的建议
Conclusion	• Add a concluding statement and express a wish or hope about the situation

Note that in all cases, you should support any advantages or disadvantages that you mention or advice that you give with clear and relevant reasons, details, and examples.

Test Expert Speaking Practice *for* **CELPIP**®

Task 1 – Step-By-Step Guide

Following these five steps will help you deliver great responses to Task 1 questions.

BEFORE YOU SPEAK

STEP 1 Begin by reading the topic carefully. Decide which type of question it is. This will help you decide how to organize your response most effectively. For example, do you need to advise somebody about the better of two choices, or discuss the advantages and disadvantages of doing something, or give advice to somebody about how to do something well? The preparation time is short, so finish this step as quickly as you can.

STEP 2 Brainstorm what you will say in your response. Remember that you should support your advice with reasons and supporting details or examples, so make sure you brainstorm these as well.

You may wish to write down your ideas. You will not have time to write in full sentences, so write in note form only. You may wish to number the points in your notes in the order you will say them.

1.
2.

WHILE YOU SPEAK

STEP 3 When the recording time begins, deliver your response. Try to speak clearly and avoid speaking either too quickly or too slowly. Pause briefly after each sentence, but try to avoid long pauses or hesitations in the middle of your sentences because these might reduce your score. Follow your notes, if you have them, so that you remember what you want to say and in what order.

When you are speaking, keep an eye on how much time is remaining. If you see that you are running out of time, start speaking slightly more quickly.

STEP 4 After you have finished your response, check how much time is remaining.

如果时间有剩

If there is a lot of time remaining, you can fill the time by saying something like "I hope that what I have said is useful. If you would like to discuss more, why don't you call me at home this evening? I think you know my telephone number." 解私明间剩太多

If there is little time remaining, it is usually best just to be silent and *not* say anything else.

AFTER YOU SPEAK

relax

STEP 5 Use the time before the next task begins first to take a deep breath. This will help you relax. Then think about what you will need to do in the next task. This will help you prepare more quickly and be ready to use the preparation time as effectively as possible.

Task 1 – Common Mistakes

Some common mistakes that test-takers make in Task 1 include the following:

Lack of Supporting Reasons and/or Examples

As a general rule, the advice you give the other person is not as important as your reason(s) for giving that advice and the details and examples that help the listener understand why your advice is likely to be helpful.

★ To avoid this problem, try to give your advice clearly in just one or two sentences. Then explain why this is your advice in at least two or three sentences, or more if possible. In other words, you should spend more time explaining *why* something is your advice than saying *what* your advice is.

Repetition of Ideas

Many test-takers find it hard to come up with ideas. As a result, they often repeat the same idea two or even three times. This is likely to reduce their overall score.

★ To avoid this problem, make sure you include plenty of supporting details and examples for each idea. One effective way to do this is to answer "unspoken questions" that the listener might have. For example, if the advice you want to give is that asking questions is a good way to be successful in a job interview, you could include answers to the following unspoken questions in your response: why asking questions is a good idea; when to ask questions; how often to ask questions; what kinds of questions to ask; and so on.

Task 1 – Useful Language

There are many things you might need to say in a response to a Task 1 question. Here are some functions with example expressions that are likely to be useful:

Making a Recommendation	• If I were you, I would … • Have you considered … ?	• You could … • In my view, you should …
Giving a reason	• One reason is that … • This is because …	• Why? Well, … • The main reason is that …
Giving an example	• For example, … • For instance, …	• such as … • including …
Expressing Benefits or Problems	• One benefit of this is that … • This is good because …	• One issue is that … • This might be a problem because …

Task 1 – Sample Response with Analysis

> *Read the prompt and the model response by a test expert. Then read the analysis of the response. This will help you understand how to give effective, high-scoring responses to Task 1 questions.*

Task 1: Giving Advice	Preparation Time: **30 seconds** Recording Time: **90 seconds**

 A friend is giving an important presentation tomorrow. Give your friend some advice about how to give a good presentation.

Hi, Sarah. I understand you're giving an important presentation soon. I often give presentations, so perhaps I can give you some helpful suggestions.

In the introduction, it is a good idea to use the name of the person you are speaking to, and to speak directly to him or her. It is also good to say why you think you can offer helpful advice.

First, I strongly recommend that you practice giving your talk several times before the day of your actual presentation. There are a couple of reasons why I recommend this. First, practicing will help you deliver your presentation in a natural way, and this is good for your audience. In addition, it will give you confidence. Whenever I have to present a talk, I always feel much more confident when I have had a chance to practice it.

In the first body section, give a clear, simple recommendation. Then supports this with one or two reasons. Notice how the speaker signposts the reasons with words like "First, …" and "In addition, …" Notice also how the speaker refers to his own experience in the last sentence. This adds support for his recommendation.

Second, don't forget to smile and use gestures when you talk. Why? Well, as I'm sure you've heard before, smiling and using gestures can help other people better understand what you're saying. If I were you, I would practice my talk in front of a mirror. This will not only help you recognize when to smile, but also when to use gestures and what kinds of gestures to use.

In the second body section, give a second clear, simple suggestion and support it with a reason and details or examples. Notice how the speaker follows the reason by suggesting how his friend could practice the recommendation.

Anyway, good luck with your presentation. I'm sure you're going to do a great job!

In the conclusion, use a word like "Anyway, …" to indicate that you have finished giving advice. Then use natural language to end your response, perhaps by wishing your friend good luck or saying that you think he or she will do a good job.

This model response has excellent coherence and meaning, good lexical range, high comprehensibility, and great task fulfillment. **If you could deliver a response like this with clear pronunciation and natural rhythm and intonation, you would probably score 11 – 12.**

Task 1 – Practice 1.1

Read these two responses to a Task 1 topic. Which response, A or B, is the better one? Why?
When you have decided, check your answers on page 106.

Task 1: Giving Advice	Preparation Time: **30 seconds** Recording Time: **90 seconds**

 A family member is deciding where to go on vacation. She will either go somewhere in Canada or somewhere in the United States. Give her some advice about where to go.

Response A

> Hi, Sarah. I heard you're going on vacation soon. That's great! I hope you have a wonderful time.
>
> Where are you going to go? Canada is a beautiful country, and there are a lot of amazing places to visit. I had a great time in Niagara Falls last year. Of course, I also had a wonderful time when I visited New York.
>
> I was at a bookstore last week and I saw a book about the Rocky Mountains. They look beautiful. Did you know that the Rocky Mountains are in the USA as well as in Canada? I would love to visit them, if I can.
>
> Anyway, I hope you have a fantastic time. I haven't had a vacation for a couple of years, so I'm jealous!

Response B

> Hi, Sarah. I understand you're taking a vacation soon either in Canada or in the USA. I took a holiday in both countries last year, so perhaps I can give you some helpful advice.
>
> I strongly recommend that you go on vacation somewhere in Canada. Not only is Canada a beautiful country, but there are many amazing places you can go. If you want to stay in Ontario, for instance, you could go to Niagara Falls. Or if you prefer another province, the mountains and forests in British Columbia and Alberta or the beaches and seafood on Prince Edward Island are all incredible.
>
> I don't recommend going to the USA, though. The exchange rate with the US dollar is not good right now, so going there would be pretty expensive. Currently, you get just 70 cents for each Canadian dollar. This means that everything will be about 30 percent more expensive in the USA than in Canada. I've heard that the economy is not likely to improve soon, so I doubt the exchange rate will improve either.
>
> Anyway, wherever you decide to go on your vacation, I really hope that you have a wonderful time.

▶ Now practice the better response until you can say it naturally and fluently in 90 seconds or less.

Test Expert Speaking Practice *for* CELPIP®

Task 1 – Practice 1.2

This response to a Task 1 topic has some missing phrases. Choose the phrase from the list that best completes each blank and write it in the space. Then check the completed response on page 106.

Task 1: Giving Advice	Preparation Time: **30 seconds**	Recording Time: **90 seconds**

> ⓘ One of your friends is thinking about quitting his job and going back to college. Advise him on the advantages and disadvantages of doing this.

Hi, David. I understand that you're thinking about quitting your job and going back to college to study.
1 _As you know_ , I did that a few years ago, so perhaps I can give you some advice.

On the one hand, there are definitely some benefits to your plan. **2** ~~On the other hand~~ *for one thing* improving your education may help you in the future. Getting an MBA **3** _definitely helped me_ find a really great job because employers wanted somebody with an advanced qualification. And for another thing, I know that you really dislike your current position at ABC Industries, so maybe a career change **4** _would be good_ for you.

5 ~~for one thing~~ ~~on the other hand~~ *on the other hand* , there are some possible drawbacks to your idea. First, the economy may not be in a good state in the future. As a result, **6** _you might find_ it hard to get a job after you graduate from college. **7** _and second_ , college fees are high right now. This means that you might be in financial trouble if you decide to go back to school.

Anyway, **8** _whatever you decide_ to do, I'm sure you'll have a lot of success in the future.

Phrases

and second	definitely helped me	for one thing	would be good
as you know	on the other hand	whatever you decide	you might find

▶ **Now practice the completed response until you can say it naturally and fluently in 90 seconds or less.**

Task 1 – Practice 1.3

> *This response to a Task 1 topic has a number of grammar and vocabulary mistakes. A test expert has crossed out the errors. Write in the corrections. Then check the corrected response on page 106.*

Task 1: Giving Advice	Preparation Time: **30 seconds** Recording Time: **90 seconds**

> ℹ️ The daughter of a family friend wants to improve his health. She has asked for your advice about easy ways that she could do this. Suggest different things she could do.

Hi, Sarah. I understand ~~your~~ **1** *you're* interested in becoming healthier. I really tried to improve my health last year, so perhaps I can give you some helpful ~~advise~~ **2** *advice* .

First, if I were you, I would try to eat healthy food, ~~specially~~ **3** *especially* fruits and vegetables. I read an interesting article about this topic last year. ~~According~~ **4** *According to* what I read, eating plenty of fruits and vegetables can help one lose ~~the weight~~ **5** *weight* and stay healthy. I started trying to eat more healthily last year, and since then, I've lost five kilograms and have hardly been sick at all. Perhaps you'll have the same results as me.

Second, have you considered doing ~~regularly~~ **6** *regular* ~~route~~ exercise in the park that is ~~nearby~~ **7** ~~close to~~ *near* your home? That park has a running track, a cycle path, and a public swimming pool, so you could do a variety of different types of workouts. The track and path are free, I ~~am~~ ~~believe~~ **8** ~~& think~~ *believe* , and the pool is inexpensive at just $5 per time, so exercising there wouldn't cost you a lot.

Anyway, whatever you decide to do, good luck! I sincerely hope that you achieve your goal of becoming healthier.

▶ **Now practice the corrected response until you can say it naturally and fluently in 90 seconds or less.**

Test Expert Speaking Practice *for* **CELPIP**®

Task 1 – Practice 1.4

Write your own response to this Task 1 topic using the responses on the previous pages as a guide. After you finish writing your response, compare it with the suggested response on page 107.

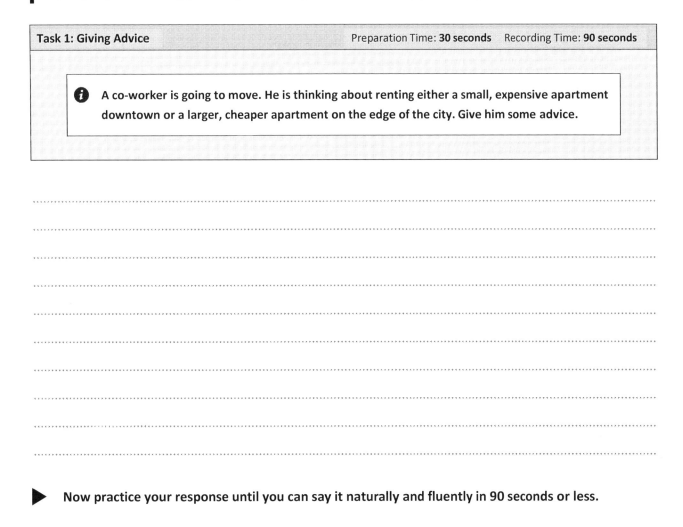

Task 1: Giving Advice   Preparation Time: **30 seconds**   Recording Time: **90 seconds**

ⓘ A co-worker is going to move. He is thinking about renting either a small, expensive apartment downtown or a larger, cheaper apartment on the edge of the city. Give him some advice.

▶ Now practice your response until you can say it naturally and fluently in 90 seconds or less.

Task 1 – Practice 1.5

Prepare and deliver a response to this Task 1 topic under test conditions. Record your response, if possible. Then listen critically to the recording. Make a list of ways you could improve your response.

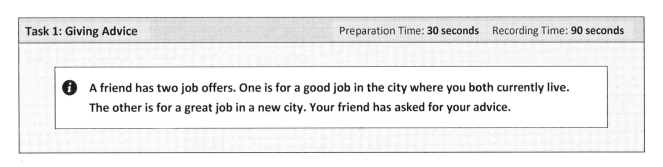

Task 1: Giving Advice   Preparation Time: **30 seconds**   Recording Time: **90 seconds**

ⓘ A friend has two job offers. One is for a good job in the city where you both currently live. The other is for a great job in a new city. Your friend has asked for your advice.

SPEAKING TASK 2

Task 2 – Introduction

After Task 1, the computer will automatically move on to the next question. Task 2 questions ask you to talk about a personal experience related to a common or everyday situation. **You will have 30 seconds in which to prepare your response, and 60 seconds in which to deliver your response.**

In most cases, the topic will give you describe a situation and then give you some examples of things you could talk about. You can talk about the examples, if you like, or you can discuss your own example of an experience that matches the situation. You can even make up a realistic example and talk about something that did not really happen. The topic will also include some questions, such as what, why, and where.

Your focus in Task 2 should be to describe events and experiences in a clear, logical, well-organized way and to answer the questions. As with every speaking task, there is no right answer or preferred response.

During the **preparation time** for Task 2, the computer screen will look something like this:

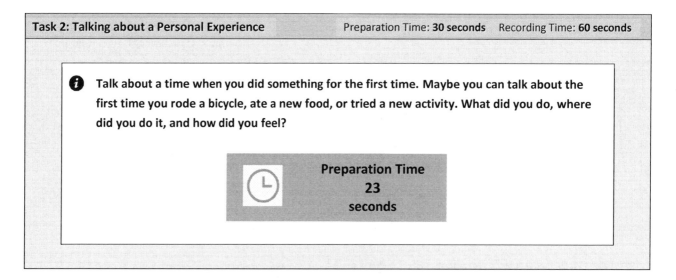

At the top of the screen, you will see the title bar, which shows the speaking task you are currently doing, how much time you have to prepare, and how much time you have in which to speak.

In the middle of the screen, you will see the topic. Below the topic, you will see a timer. This will count down until there is no more preparation time remaining.

Test Expert Speaking Practice *for* **CELPIP**®

After the preparation time has finished, the computer will automatically go on to the recording screen, which will look similar to this:

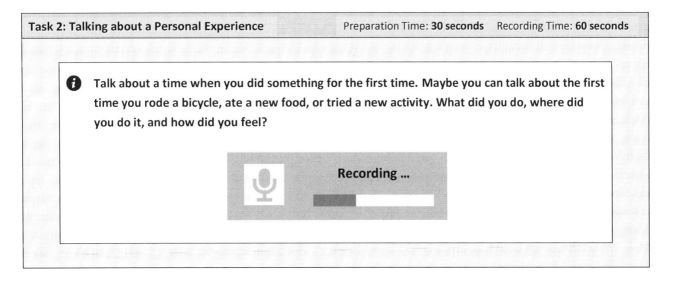

In the middle of the screen you will see an icon of a microphone as well as a bar showing the amount of time remaining in which to record your response. As soon as you see this screen, you should begin speaking. The computer will automatically record what you say. You do not need to click anything to start recording.

After the recording time is up, the computer will stop recording automatically. The screen will change and look similar to this:

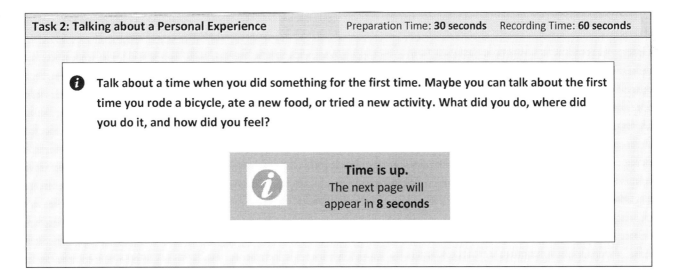

When the computer stops recording, it will automatically save your response. You do not need to click anything to save the response. After a few seconds, the computer will automatically go on to Task 3.

Task 2 – How to Organize Your Response

Every Task 2 topic asks you to talk about a different personal experience, but the topics usually follow a standard pattern. As a result, you can use the same basic organization for your response regardless of the topic.

In general, a good response to a Task 2 question will have the following organization and include the following information.

Introduction	• Mention that you have had several experiences that match the topic • Say that you will talk about one particular experience
Body of Speech	• Describe an experience that matches the topic • Give relevant details and examples that also match the topic; make sure your response includes answers to the questions that the topic asks
Conclusion	Add a concluding statement that summarizes your experience

During the body of your speech, there are various ways you can organize the things you say. Some methods of organizing your ideas that are especially useful for Task 2 include:

• Sequential Order

When you organize your ideas using a sequential order, you mention each thing, event, or point in the order in which it happened. In other words, you talk about each event in sequence.

So, for example, if the Task 2 topic asks you to talk about a party you attended, you might first talk about getting ready for the party, then mention how you went to the party, then say what happened at the party, before finally discussing how you felt after the party.

Chronological order is similar to sequential order. The difference is that when using chronological order, you talk about details in time order. This is usually from earliest (or first) to latest (or last).

• Topical Order

When you organize your ideas using a topical order, you discuss two or more smaller topics that are related to an overall topic.

So, for instance, if the Task 2 topic asks you to talk about a party you attended, you might first talk about the food you ate at the party, then discuss the other people who were at the party, before finally mentioning some of the interesting conversations you had with those people.

Test Expert Speaking Practice *for* **CELPIP**®

Task 2 – Step-By-Step Guide

Following these five steps will help you deliver great responses to Task 2 questions.

BEFORE YOU SPEAK

STEP 1   Begin by reading the topic carefully. Make sure you understand any specific details that the topic asks you to speak about. For example, do you have to discuss something you did *when you were a child*, or something that you have done *just once*? If you are not careful about specific details like this and talk about something you did when you were an adult, for example, it may affect your score. As always, be sure to complete this step as quickly as possible.

STEP 2   Brainstorm what experience you will talk about in your response. Make sure you choose an experience that is easy for you to talk about, easy for the raters to understand, and matches the topic. Also brainstorm relevant details and examples you can include in your response.

You may wish to write down your ideas. You will not have time to write in full sentences, so write in note form only. You may wish to number the points in your notes in the order you will say them.

WHILE YOU SPEAK

STEP 3   When the recording time begins, deliver your response. Try to speak clearly and avoid speaking either too quickly or too slowly. Pause briefly after each sentence, but try to avoid long pauses or hesitations in the middle of your sentences because these might reduce your score. Follow your notes, if you have them, so that you remember what you want to say and in what order.

When you are speaking, keep an eye on how much time is remaining. If you see that you are running out of time, start speaking slightly more quickly.

STEP 4   After you have finished your response, check how much time is remaining.

If there is a lot of time remaining, you can fill the time by saying something like "I would love to have another experience like this in the future" or "I hope one day I can share an experience similar to this with my spouse and kids."

If there is little time remaining, it is usually best just to be silent and *not* say anything else.

AFTER YOU SPEAK

STEP 5   Use the time before the next task begins first to take a deep breath. This will help you relax. Then think about what you will need to do in the next task. This will help you prepare more quickly and be ready to use the preparation time as effectively as possible.

Task 2 - Common Mistakes

Some common mistakes that test-takers make in Task 2 include the following:

Unclear Organization

If your response is not clearly organized, the raters may find it hard to understand your ideas. In addition, an unclear organization makes it more likely you will repeat ideas. Both of these things may affect your score.

★ To avoid this problem, decide how to organize your response during the brainstorming stage and follow this organization as you speak. Then help the raters understand your organization by using clear signpost words.

Poor Choice of Experience to Discuss

The experience you choose to talk about should match two criteria: it should be something that is obviously related to the topic, and it should be something you have talked about before (preferably in English). If you choose to talk about something that is only indirectly related to the topic, the raters may be confused. And if you discuss something you have rarely or never discussed before, it will be more difficult for you to speak about the topic and you are more likely to make mistakes. Both of these things may affect your score.

★ To avoid this problem, always choose to talk about experiences that are obviously related to the topic and that you have talked about before. If you cannot think of any experiences that match both of these criteria, remember that there is no penalty for talking about an imaginary experience.

Task 2 - Useful Language

There are many things you might need to say in a response to a Task 2 question. Here are some functions with example expressions that are likely to be useful:

Talking about events in sequence	• First, ... • Then ...	• After that, ... • Finally, ...
Saying when something happened	• It happened in [month / year] ... • When I was a child, ...	• A few (days / weeks / etc.) ago, ... • Recently, ...
Adding some additional information	• In addition, ... • Moreover, ...	• Another (thing / idea / etc.) ... • I should also mention that ...
Saying how something made you feel	• This made me feel really ... • I was (excited / happy / etc.) ...	• Afterwards, I felt ... • I (have / had) never felt more ...

Task 2 – Sample Response with Analysis

Read the prompt and the model response by a test expert. Then read the analysis of the response. This will help you understand how to give effective, high-scoring responses to Task 2 questions.

Task 2: Talking about a Personal Experience	Preparation Time: **30 seconds**	Recording Time: **60 seconds**

 Talk about a time when you did something for the first time. Maybe you can talk about the first time you rode a bicycle, ate a new food, or tried a new activity. What did you do, where did you do it, and how did you feel?

In my life, I have done many things for the first time. If I had to pick just one thing to talk about, however, it would be the first time I ate sushi.

It happened a few years ago. Some of my friends wanted to go out for sushi. I was nervous, because I didn't like fish, but I decided to go with them. My friends ordered some plates of sushi for us all to share. The first one I tried was salmon sushi. I was worried that it would taste bad, but actually it was delicious. After that, I tried some shrimp sushi. That was delicious, too. In fact, I liked them both so much that I ordered more!

Eating sushi made me feel really great, and since that first time, I have eaten it regularly.

In the introduction, it is a good idea to use an opening sentence to refer to other experiences that match the topic. You should then clearly state which experience you will talk about.

In the body section, describe the events in a clear, organized way. Include relevant and believable details and examples. Make sure that you answer all of the questions in the prompt.

In this case, notice how the speaker describes the events in sequential order and gives specific details about the different types of sushi he ate and how much he liked them.

In the conclusion, summarize your experience. You can also mention how often you have had a similar experience or if / when you would like to have the same experience in the future.

In this case, notice how the speaker also uses the conclusion to answer the question in the prompt about how the experience made him feel.

This model response has excellent coherence and meaning, good lexical range, high comprehensibility, and great task fulfillment. **If you could deliver a response like this with clear pronunciation and natural rhythm and intonation, you would probably score 11 – 12.**

Task 2 – Practice 2.1

Read these two responses to a Task 2 topic. Which response, A or B, is the better one? Why? When you have decided, check your answers on page 107.

Task 2: Talking about a Personal Experience Preparation Time: **30 seconds** Recording Time: **60 seconds**

 Talk about a time when you learned something after making a mistake. Maybe you can talk about what you learned after having an argument with a friend, or what you learned after forgetting something important. What mistake did you make and what did you learn from it?

Response A

In my life, I have learned from my mistakes a number of times. If I had to pick just one thing to talk about, however, it would be the time when I failed an exam.

It happened when I was at high school. I had an important history exam coming up, but I also had a part-time job. I wanted to make some money to buy a video game, so instead of studying hard for my exam, I worked every evening. Of course, I ended up failing the exam because of my mistake in not studying.

Failing the exam made me feel really bad. I learned that it's better to study and do well at school than to spend time on things that don't really matter – like working part-time just in order to buy video games.

Response B

In my life, I have learned from my mistakes a number of times. If I had to pick just one thing to talk about, however, it would be the time when I had a big argument with my brother.

It happened about 15 years ago. My brother wanted to watch a baseball game on TV, but I wanted to watch a movie. At first, we discussed what to watch in a friendly way, but soon we both became angry. We were so mad, in fact, that we didn't speak to each other for several days after that.

If I think about it now, I should have let my brother watch the baseball game. It was an important game, and baseball was one of his favourite activities, and the movie I wanted to watch wasn't a very good one.

▶ **Now practice the better response until you can say it naturally and fluently in 60 seconds or less.**

Test Expert Speaking Practice *for* **CELPIP**®

Task 2 – Practice 2.2

> *This response to a Task 2 topic has some missing phrases. Choose the phrase from the list that best completes each blank and write it in the space. Then check the completed response on page 107.*

Task 2: Talking about a Personal Experience	Preparation Time: **30 seconds**	Recording Time: **60 seconds**

> ℹ️ Talk about a time when you had to make a difficult choice. Maybe you can talk about choosing where to live, what job to do, or what subject to study at college. What choice did you make, why was it a difficult one, and how do you feel about your choice now?

In my life, I have had to make difficult choices several times. If I had to pick **1** _____
to talk about, however, it would be deciding **2** _____ *to help my friend.*

A couple of years ago, my friend James was **3** _____ *. One month, he needed $1000 to pay his rent, and he asked* **4** _____ *borrow it from me. I really wanted to help him. However, my parents* **5** _____ *not to lend money to friends, so I said no to James. He said that he understood and that* **6** _____ *friends, but actually we stopped seeing each other* **7** _____ *.*

8 _____ *, I miss spending time with James, so I wish that I had loaned him the money he needed.*

Phrases

after that	if he could	just one example	we would still be
always told me	in financial difficulties	to be honest	whether or not

▶ **Now practice the completed response until you can say it naturally and fluently in 60 seconds or less.**

Task 2 – Practice 2.3

This response to a Task 2 topic has a number of grammar and vocabulary mistakes. A test expert has crossed out the errors. Write in the corrections. Then check the corrected response on page 107.

Task 2: Talking about a Personal Experience	Preparation Time: **30 seconds** Recording Time: **60 seconds**

> ℹ️ **Talk about a time when you had a surprising experience. Maybe you can talk about meeting somebody unexpectedly or finding out some surprising news. What was the experience, why was it surprising, and how did you feel about it at the time?**

In my life, I have had surprising experiences ~~number of~~ **1** _____ times. If I had to pick just one example to talk about, however, it would be winning a scholarship to ~~go~~ **2** _____ a conference.

It happened just ~~few~~ **3** _____ weeks ago. I saw an article online about a conference in Australia. The article ~~told~~ **4** _____ that one person could win a scholarship to attend. I've always wanted to ~~visit to~~ **5** _____ Australia and the conference sounded interesting, so I decided to apply. However, the deadline was in just a few hours, so I had to complete the application extremely ~~quick~~ **6** _____ .

I thought that I had no chance, so I was ~~both of~~ **7** _____ surprised and pleased when I found out that I had won! Now, however, I'm nervous ~~because of~~ **8** _____ I have to speak in front of hundreds of people.

▶ **Now practice the corrected response until you can say it naturally and fluently in 60 seconds or less.**

Task 2 – Practice 2.4

Write your own response to this Task 2 topic using the responses on the previous pages as a guide. After you finish writing your response, compare it with the suggested response on page 108.

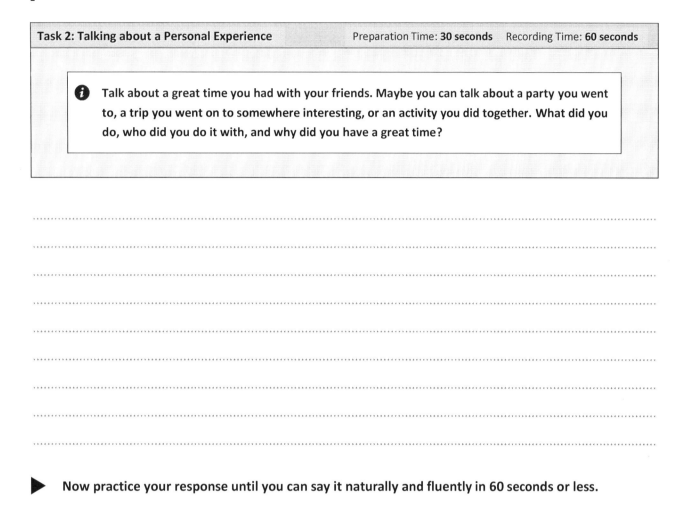

Task 2: Talking about a Personal Experience   Preparation Time: **30 seconds**   Recording Time: **60 seconds**

> **ℹ** Talk about a great time you had with your friends. Maybe you can talk about a party you went to, a trip you went on to somewhere interesting, or an activity you did together. What did you do, who did you do it with, and why did you have a great time?

▶ Now practice your response until you can say it naturally and fluently in 60 seconds or less.

Task 2 – Practice 2.5

Prepare and deliver a response to this Task 2 topic under test conditions. Record your response, if possible. Then listen critically to the recording. Make a list of ways you could improve your response.

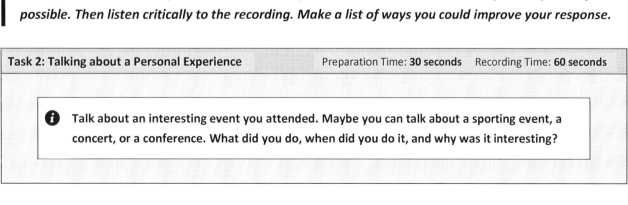

Task 2: Talking about a Personal Experience   Preparation Time: **30 seconds**   Recording Time: **60 seconds**

> **ℹ** Talk about an interesting event you attended. Maybe you can talk about a sporting event, a concert, or a conference. What did you do, when did you do it, and why was it interesting?

SPEAKING TASK 3

Task 3 – Introduction

After Task 2, the computer will automatically move on to the next question. Task 3 questions ask you to describe some of the things you can see in a picture. Generally speaking, the picture will show people interacting with one another in a common setting. You have to imagine that you are talking to somebody who cannot see the picture. **You will have 30 seconds in which to prepare your response, and 60 seconds in which to deliver your response.**

Your focus in Task 3 should be to give a clear description of what you can see. You need to give enough detail that the other person can imagine the picture. You do not have to talk about everything you can see in the picture, and as with every speaking task, there is no right answer or preferred response.

During the **preparation time** for Task 3, the computer screen will look something like this.

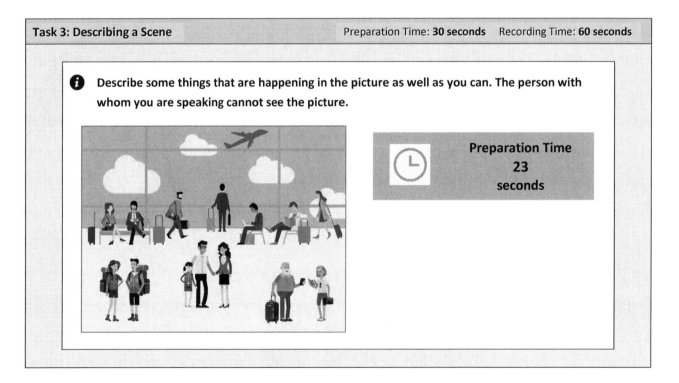

| Task 3: Describing a Scene | Preparation Time: **30 seconds**   Recording Time: **60 seconds** |

> ℹ️ Describe some things that are happening in the picture as well as you can. The person with whom you are speaking cannot see the picture.
>
> Preparation Time
> 23
> seconds

At the top of the screen, you will see the title bar, which shows the speaking task you are currently doing, how much time you have to prepare, and how much time you have in which to speak.

In the middle of the screen, you will see the topic and the picture. (Note that you can see a larger version of all the pictures in the Task 3 section in the Picture Appendix, which starts on page 118.) Next to the picture, you will see a clock icon and a timer, which will count down until there is no preparation time left.

After the preparation time, the computer will automatically go on to the recording screen:

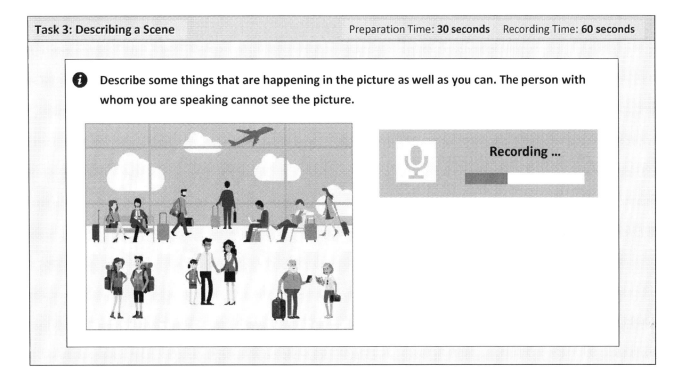

Next to the picture, you will see an icon of a microphone and a bar showing the amount of time remaining in which to record your response. As soon as you see this screen, you should begin speaking. The computer will automatically record what you say. You do not need to click anything to start recording.

After the recording time is up, the computer will stop recording automatically. The screen will change and look similar to this:

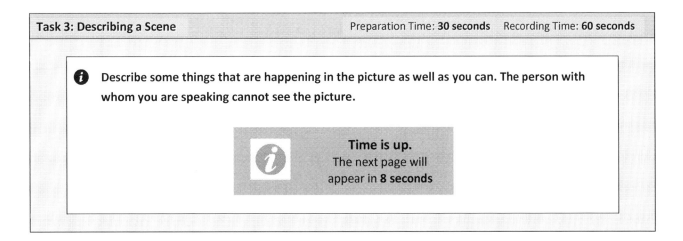

When the computer stops recording, it will automatically save your response. You do not need to click anything to save the response. After a few seconds, the computer will automatically go on to Task 4.

Task 3 – How to Organize Your Response

Every Task 3 topic shows you a different picture, but in general the pictures are similar to one another. As a result, you can use the same basic organization for your response provided that you vary the body of your speech depending on what kind of picture you get.

In general, a good response to a Task 3 question will have the following organization and include the following information.

Introduction	• Give a brief description of the overall scene of the picture • Add a transition to say that you will discuss some of the things you see
Body of Speech	• Describe some of the main things you can see in the picture; include as much detail as possible about each thing you describe; in addition, try to say either where each thing is in relation to the picture (e.g., "on the left …") or where it is in relation to something else in the picture (e.g., next to the …)
Conclusion	• Finish by stating that you did not describe everything in the picture

In the body of your speech, you should follow a logical order when you describe what you can see in the picture. Generally, you should follow one of these three approaches:

• Describe What You Can See from Left to Right

If the picture is relatively flat and most of the actions are horizontal rather than vertical, usually the best option is first to describe what you can see in the left third of the picture, then what you can see in the middle third, and finally what you can see in the right third.

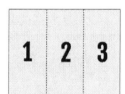

• Describe What You Can See from Top to Bottom

If the picture is relatively flat and has little depth but shows something that has vertical layers or height, the best option may be to describe what you can see in the top third of the picture, then what you can see in the middle third, and finally what you can see in the bottom third.

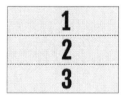

• Describe What You Can See from Foreground to Background

If the picture has depth, meaning that people and objects in the "front" of the picture are larger and appear closer to you than people and objects in the "back" of the picture, then the best option is often to describe what you can see in the foreground, then what you can see in the middle ground, and finally what you can see in the background.

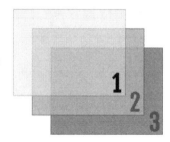

Task 3 – Step-By-Step Guide

Following these four steps will help you deliver great responses to Task 3 questions. (Note that because Task 3 questions ask you to describe a picture, you do not need to follow the usual step of carefully reading and understanding the topic.)

BEFORE YOU SPEAK

STEP 1   Look at the whole picture. Decide whether you will describe what you can see from left to right, from top to bottom, or from foreground to background. Then decide which people and things in the picture you will describe and how you will describe them.

You may find it helpful to draw a rectangle to match the picture and then to draw numbers in the same place as the things you will describe. This will help you follow the organization you decided earlier. You may also find it helpful to make notes about what you will say during the recording phase.

WHILE YOU SPEAK

STEP 2   When the recording time begins, deliver your response. Try to speak clearly and avoid speaking either too quickly or too slowly. Pause briefly after each sentence, but try to avoid long pauses or hesitations in the middle of your sentences because these might reduce your score. Follow your notes, if you have them, so that you remember what you want to say and in what order.

When you are speaking, keep an eye on how much time is remaining. If you see that you are running out of time, start speaking slightly more quickly.

STEP 3   After you have finished your response, check how much time is remaining.

If there is a lot of time left, you can fill the remaining time by saying something that matches the picture, such as "It looks like most of the people in the picture are having a great time." You could also connect the picture to your own life by saying something like, "The scene in the picture reminds me of a photograph I saw in a magazine a few months ago." Finally, you could speak directly to the listener and say something like, "I hope you can imagine the scene based on my words. Do you have any questions about what I've said?"

If there is little time remaining, it is usually best just to be silent and *not* say anything else.

AFTER YOU SPEAK

STEP 4   Use the time before the next task begins first to take a deep breath. This will help you relax. Then think about what you will need to do in the next task. This will help you prepare more quickly and be ready to use the preparation time as effectively as possible.

Task 3 – Common Mistakes

Some common mistakes that test-takers make in Task 3 include the following:

Unclear Organization or Lack of Organization

If you jump around when you describe what you can see – first talking about what you can see in the top left of the picture, for example, then the middle right, then the bottom left, and so on – the raters will find it hard to get a mental image of the picture. In addition, an unclear organization makes it more likely you will repeat ideas. Both of these things may affect your score.

★   To avoid this problem, decide how to organize your response during the preparation time and follow this organization as you speak. Also use clear expressions to say where something is in the picture.

Lack of Descriptive Details

Your job in Task 3 is to give the raters a mental image of the picture. To do this, you will need to use clear descriptive language. If you just say, for example, "There is a woman near a man," the raters will not have a clear idea of what the woman and man look like, what they are doing, and so on. In addition, you may finish your response too early because your descriptions are so short and lacking in detail.

★   To avoid this problem, use clear descriptive language when talking about what you can see. You can also use phrases to express doubt or uncertainty. These will fill the time in a natural-sounding way. For example, instead of saying "There is a woman standing near a man," you could say "There is a slim young woman standing near a young man with a beard. It looks like they are holding hands."

Task 3 – Useful Language

There are many things you might need to say in a response to a Task 3 question. Here are some functions with example expressions that are likely to be useful:

Saying where a thing is in the picture	• On the left / right of the picture ... • In the middle of ...	• At the top / bottom of ... • In the foreground / background of ...
Saying where X is in relation to Y	• ... is in front of / behind the ... • ... is next to / near the ...	• ... is just above / below the ... • ... is on top of / underneath the ...
Sounding uncertain or doubtful	• It looks like he / she might be ... • He / She seems to be ...	• I think that he / she is ... • He / she appears to be ...
Describing people	• ... thin / slender / slim / obese ... • ... young / middle-aged / old ...	• ... with glasses / a hat / a beard ... • ... with short / medium / long hair ...

Task 3 – Sample Response with Analysis

> *Read the prompt and the model response by a test expert. Then read the analysis of the response. This will help you understand how to give effective, high-scoring responses to Task 3 questions.*

Task 3: Describing a Scene	Preparation Time: **30 seconds** Recording Time: **60 seconds**

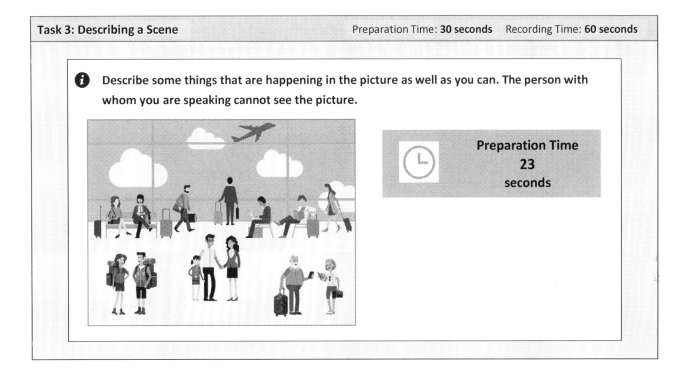

ℹ️ Describe some things that are happening in the picture as well as you can. The person with whom you are speaking cannot see the picture.

This scene shows what looks like an airport. I'll describe some of the things and people I can see in the picture and say what they're doing.

In the introduction, give a brief description of the overall scene. Then say that you will describe some of the people (and things) you can see.

In the foreground of the picture, a young couple with backpacks are talking to each other. Near them are a couple with a young daughter. And next to them are two elderly people looking at what seems to be a cellphone and a guidebook. In the background, I can see people sitting on chairs or benches reading or using laptops. Other people are walking or looking out at an airplane taking off. All the people in the background have luggage.

In the body section, describe what you can see in an organized way. In this case, the speaker first describes what he can see in the foreground of the picture and then in the background. Include details in your descriptions, and say where the people are in relation to other people or things.

There is more I could describe, but I hope this gives a clear overall impression of the scene.

In the conclusion, finish your response by saying that there are other things you could have described. Also express the hope that your response has given the listener a mental image.

This model response has excellent coherence and meaning, good lexical range, high comprehensibility, and great task fulfillment. **If you could deliver a response like this with clear pronunciation and natural rhythm and intonation, you would probably score 11 – 12.**

Task 3 – Practice 3.1

Read these three responses to a Task 3 topic. Which response, A, B, or C, is the best one? Why?
When you have decided, check your answers on page 108.

Task 3: Describing a Scene	Preparation Time: **30 seconds**	Recording Time: **60 seconds**

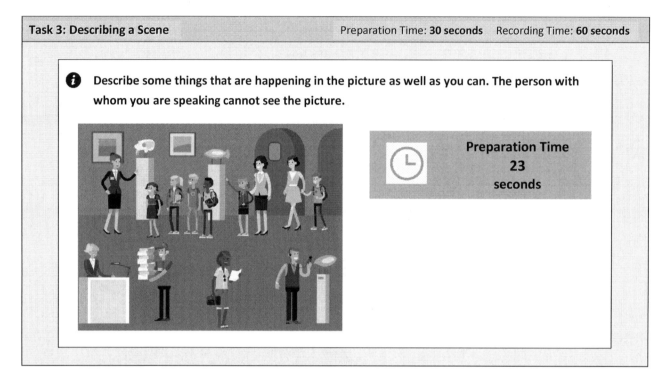

ℹ️ Describe some things that are happening in the picture as well as you can. The person with whom you are speaking cannot see the picture.

Preparation Time
23
seconds

(If you want to see the details of the picture better, remember that the Picture Appendix, which starts on page 118, has a larger version not just of this picture, but of all of the pictures in this Task 3 section.)

Test Expert Speaking Practice *for* **CELPIP**®

Response A

This scene shows what looks like a museum. Or it might be an art gallery or maybe even a shop. I'm not sure. I'll describe some of the things and people I can see in the picture and say what they're doing.

There are objects like a skull and paintings on the wall. There's a woman holding hands with a boy. There's another woman talking about something. There's a girl with her hand in the air near a woman. There are some children. There's a man carrying some boxes or something. There's another man looking at something and listening to some music or perhaps a recording. There's a woman sitting behind a desk. And there's also a woman looking at a map or guide or something.

There is more I could say, but I hope this gives a clear overall impression of the scene.

Response B

This scene is a museum. I'll describe some of the things and people I can see in the picture and say what they're doing.

On the left of the picture there are two women. One is raising her hand and talking; the other is sitting behind a desk. In the middle of the picture there is a man carrying something heavy, some children standing near a girl asking a question, and a woman reading a guidebook or looking at a map. And on the right of the picture, there is a woman holding hands with a young boy and a man standing near an object and listening to some music or something.

There is more I could mention, but I hope this gives a clear overall impression of the scene.

Response C

This scene shows what looks like a museum. I'll describe some of the things and people I can see in the picture and say what they're doing.

At the top of the picture, I can see a museum guide talking to some schoolchildren. She appears to be describing a skull. One of the schoolgirls wants to ask a question. Near this girl are a mother and son. At the bottom of the picture, I can see a delivery person carrying some boxes or books. It looks like he wants to give them to a woman sitting behind a desk. Near the delivery man there is a woman looking at a guidebook or map. And near her there is a man looking at a piece of art and listening to something.

There is more I could describe, but I hope this gives a clear overall impression of the scene.

▶ **Now practice the best response until you can say it naturally and fluently in 60 seconds or less.**

Task 3 – Practice 3.2

This response to a Task 3 topic has some missing phrases. Choose the phrase from the list that best completes each blank and write it in the space. Then check the completed response on page 108.

Task 3: Describing a Scene   Preparation Time: **30 seconds**   Recording Time: **60 seconds**

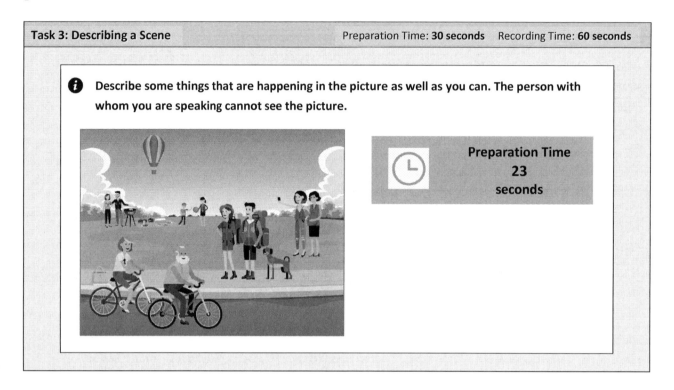

ⓘ Describe some things that are happening in the picture as well as you can. The person with whom you are speaking cannot see the picture.

Preparation Time
23
seconds

This scene shows **1** .... *a street with a park behind it. I'll describe some of the*

things and people I can see in the picture **2** .... *they're doing.*

In the foreground of the picture, two elderly people are riding bicycles. **3** .... *on*

the sidewalk are a young couple with a dog. They are wearing backpacks. **4** ....

the picture I can see two women taking a selfie. **5** .... *seems to be pregnant. In*

the background I can see a family. **6** .... *they're having a picnic. The parents are*

cooking some food on a barbecue and their two children are playing with a ball. I can see a hot air balloon

7 .... *behind them.*

There is more I could describe, but I hope this gives a clear overall impression **8** ....

Phrases

and say what	*in the sky*	*just behind them*	*one of them*
in the middle of	*it seems as if*	*of the scene*	*what looks like*

 Now practice the completed response until you can say it naturally and fluently in 60 seconds or less.

Task 3 – Practice 3.3

This response to a Task 3 topic has a number of grammar and vocabulary mistakes. A test expert has crossed out the errors. Write in the corrections. Then check the corrected response on page 109.

Task 3: Describing a Scene	Preparation Time: **30 seconds** Recording Time: **60 seconds**

ⓘ Describe some things that are happening in the picture as well as you can. The person with whom you are speaking cannot see the picture.

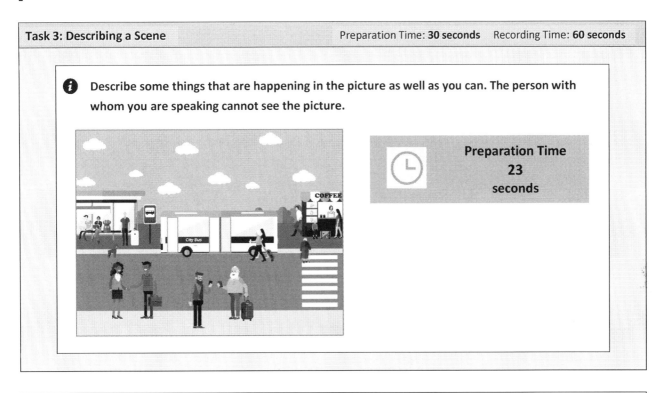

This scene ~~is showing~~ **1** .... what looks like a bus station or bus stop. I'll ~~describe about~~ **2** .... some of the things and people I can see in the picture and say what they're doing.

At the top of ~~a~~ **3** .... picture, there are people waiting in ~~the~~ **4** .... bus shelter. There is a bus near them, and some people walking ~~onto~~ **5** .... the road next to the bus. To the right of the bus, there is a café. A woman seems to be ordering a coffee. At the bottom of the picture, a man and a woman ~~shake~~ **6** .... hands. Near them I can see two men looking ~~for~~ **7** .... their phones. Both have beards, but one is young and one is older. ~~Latter~~ **8** .... has a small suitcase.

There is more I could describe, but I hope this gives a clear overall impression of the scene.

▶ Now practice the corrected response until you can say it naturally and fluently in 60 seconds or less.

Task 3 – Practice 3.4

Write your own response to this Task 3 topic using the responses on the previous pages as a guide. After you finish writing your response, compare it with the suggested response on page 109.

Task 3: Describing a Scene	Preparation Time: **30 seconds** Recording Time: **60 seconds**

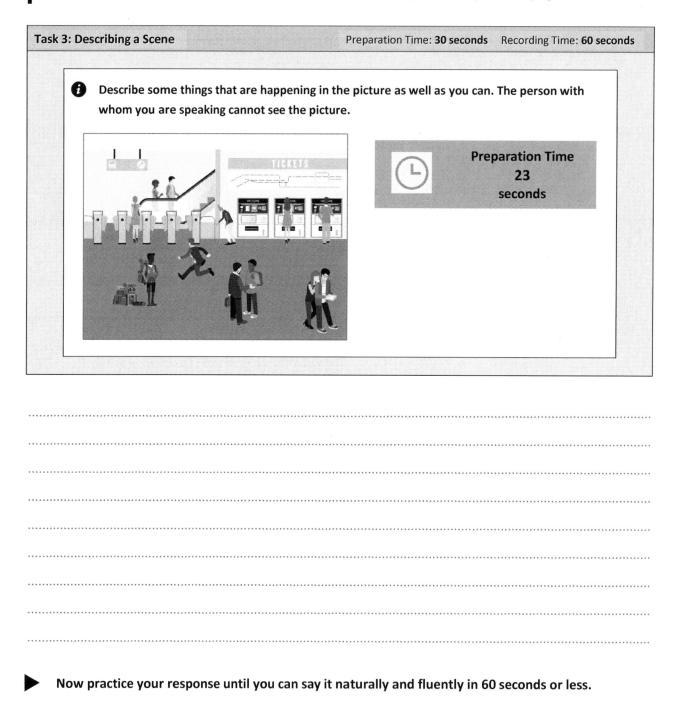

ⓘ Describe some things that are happening in the picture as well as you can. The person with whom you are speaking cannot see the picture.

Preparation Time
23
seconds

....

....

....

....

....

....

....

....

▶ Now practice your response until you can say it naturally and fluently in 60 seconds or less.

Task 3 – Practice 3.5

> *Prepare and deliver a response to this Task 3 topic under test conditions. Record your response, if possible. Then listen critically to the recording. Make a list of ways you could improve your response.*

Task 3: Describing a Scene	Preparation Time: **30 seconds** Recording Time: **60 seconds**

ℹ Describe some things that are happening in the picture as well as you can. The person with whom you are speaking cannot see the picture.

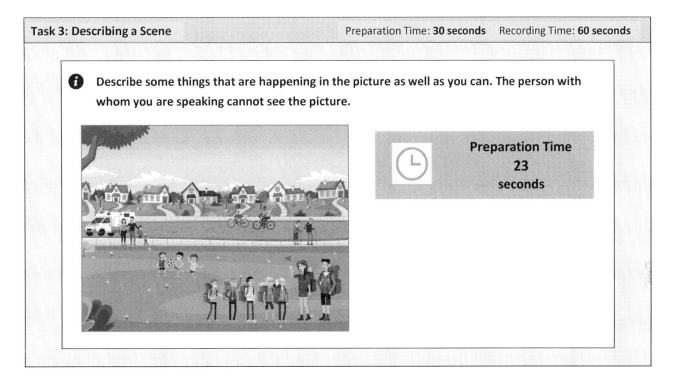

(If you want to see the details of the picture better, remember that the Picture Appendix, which starts on page 118, has a larger version not just of this picture, but of all of the pictures in this Task 3 section.)

SPEAKING TASK 4

Task 4 – Introduction

After Task 3, the computer will automatically move on to the next question. For Task 4 questions, you will see the same picture as in Task 3, and must predict what might happen next or what the people in the picture might do next. As with Task 3, you should imagine you are talking to a person who cannot see the picture. **You will have 30 seconds in which to prepare your response, and 60 seconds in which to deliver it.**

Your focus in Task 4 should be to explain what you think the people might do or what is likely to happen next. Discuss things that you think are likely based on what often happens in real life. If possible, support your predictions with a reason. You do not have to make a prediction about everything you can see in the picture. And as with every speaking task, there is no right answer or preferred response.

During the **preparation time** for Task 4, the computer screen will look something like this.

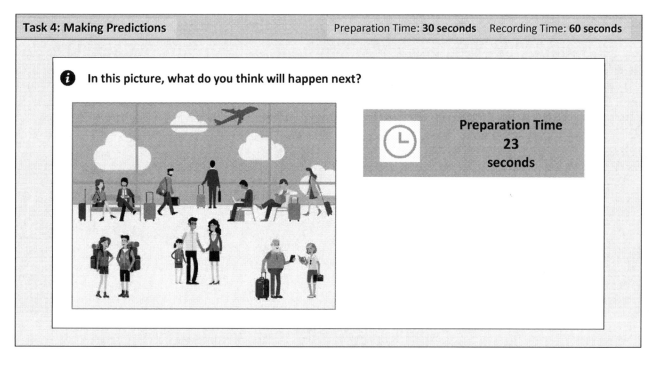

At the top of the screen, you will see the title bar, which shows the speaking task you are currently doing, how much time you have to prepare, and how much time you have in which to speak.

In the middle of the screen, you will see the topic and the picture. (Note that you can see a larger version of this and every picture in the Task 4 section in the Picture Appendix, which starts on page 118.) You will see a clock icon and timer next to the picture. The timer will count down until there is no preparation time left.

           Test Expert Speaking Practice *for* **CELPIP**®

After the preparation time, the computer will automatically go on to the recording screen:

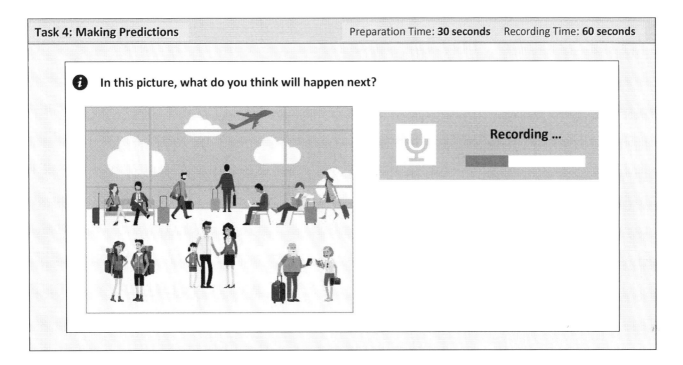

Next to the picture, you will see an icon of a microphone and a bar showing the amount of time remaining in which to record your response. As soon as you see this screen, you should begin speaking. The computer will automatically record what you say. You do not need to click anything to start recording.

After the recording time is up, the computer will stop recording automatically. The screen will change and look similar to this:

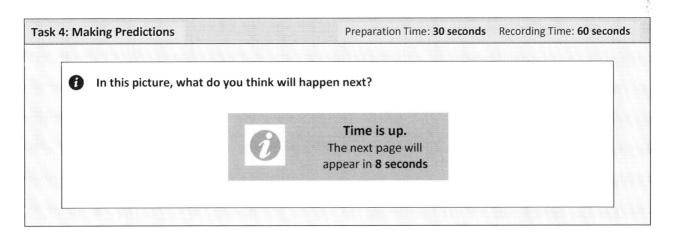

When the computer stops recording, it will automatically save your response. You do not need to click anything to save the response. After a few seconds, the computer will automatically go on to Task 4.

Task 4 – How to Organize Your Response

Every Task 4 topic shows you the same picture as the one you saw in Task 3. As a result, you can use the same basic organization for your response provided that you vary the body of your speech depending on what kind of picture you get.

In general, a good response to a Task 4 question will have the following organization and include the following information.

Introduction	• Say that you will make predictions about what might happen next (If possible, add a brief mention of where the scene is taking place)
Body of Speech	• Give predictions about what might happen to the people in the picture or what they might do; include details in your predictions, and provide reasons for your predictions, if possible
Conclusion	• Finish by stating that you are not sure if any of your predictions are accurate

In the body of your speech, you should follow a logical order when you make predictions about what will happen next or what the people will do next. There are three common ways to approach this. You should use the same approach that you used in Task 3:

- **Make Predictions from Left to Right**

If the picture is relatively flat and most of the actions are horizontal rather than vertical, usually the best option is first to make predictions about what you can see in the left third of the picture, then what you can see in the middle third, and finally what you can see in the right third.

- **Make Predictions from Top to Bottom**

If the picture is relatively flat and has little depth but shows something that has vertical layers or height, the best option may be to make predictions about what you can see in the top third of the picture, then what you can see in the middle third, and finally what you can see in the bottom third.

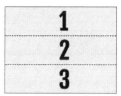

- **Make Predictions from Foreground to Background**

If the picture has depth, meaning that people and objects in the "front" of the picture are larger and appear closer to you than people and objects in the "back" of the picture, then the best option is often to make predictions about what you can see in the foreground, then what you can see in the middle ground, and finally what you can see in the background.

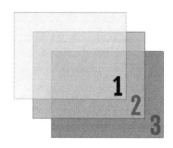

Task 4 – Step-By-Step Guide

Following these four steps will help you deliver great responses to Task 4 questions. (Note that because Task 4 questions use the same picture as Task 3 questions, just like with Task 3, you can skip one of the usual five steps.)

BEFORE YOU SPEAK

STEP 1   Decide what predictions you will make about the picture. It is a good idea to remember the order in which you described things in Task 3 and to use the same order when you you're your predictions in Task 4. (If you drew a rectangle with numbers in it as part of your preparation for Task 3, use the same rectangle to guide your response to Task 4.)

You may find it helpful to make notes about what you will say during the recording phase.

WHILE YOU SPEAK

STEP 2   When the recording time begins, deliver your response. Try to speak clearly and avoid speaking either too quickly or too slowly. Pause briefly after each sentence, but try to avoid long pauses or hesitations in the middle of your sentences because these might reduce your score. Follow your notes, if you have them, so that you remember what you want to say and in what order.

When you are speaking, keep an eye on how much time is remaining. If you see that you are running out of time, start speaking slightly more quickly.

STEP 3   After you have finished your response, check how much time is remaining.

If there is a lot of time left, you can fill the remaining time by saying something like "There are many other things that might happen, of course, but I think the ones I've mentioned are the most likely" or "Of course, other people might make different predictions if they were to look at this picture."

If there is little time remaining, it is usually best just to be silent and *not* say anything else.

AFTER YOU SPEAK

STEP 4   Use the time before the next task begins first to take a deep breath. This will help you relax. Then think about what you will need to do in the next task. This will help you prepare more quickly and be ready to use the preparation time as effectively as possible.

Task 4 – Common Mistakes

Some common mistakes that test-takers make in Task 4 include the following:

Sounding Too Certain

Your job in Task 4 is to give a prediction about what *might* happen next or what the people in the scene *might* do next. In other words, your task is *not* to talk about what will definitely happen, but about what could *possibly* happen. If you use language that sounds too certain, your response will sound unnatural, and this may affect your score.

★ To avoid this problem, you can use modals that suggest possibility, like "could," "may" or "might." You can also use verbs that suggest you are not certain, like "suspect," "feel," or "imagine." Finally, you can state directly in your conclusion that you are not sure that your predictions will come true.

Using Repetitive Language

Another potential problem is using repetitive language when making your predictions. If you always use "will" or "might" or "possibly," the raters will judge your use of language be repetitive, and this is likely to affect your score.

★ To avoid this problem, use a wide variety of natural expressions to make your predictions.

Task 4 – Useful Language

There are many things you might need to say in a response to a Task 4 question. Here are some functions with example expressions that are likely to be useful:

Introducing an opinion about something	• I think that … • I suspect that …	• I imagine that … • I feel that …
Predicting what might happen	• … is likely to … • … might very well …	• … looks as if he / she is about to … • … will probably …
Saying what people are doing / where they are	• … who is standing by / sitting on … • … who is talking to / chatting to …	• … who is walking / running … • … who is near / by / next to …
Giving a reason for a prediction	• … because … • … since …	• … because of … • … due to …

Task 4 – Sample Response with Analysis

> *Read the prompt and the model response by a test expert. Then read the analysis of the response.*
> *This will help you understand how to give effective, high-scoring responses to Task 4 questions.*

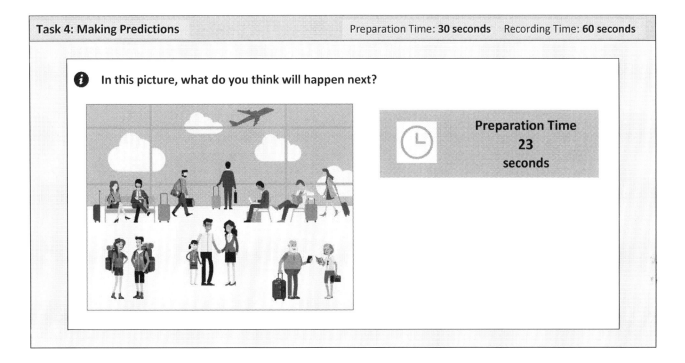

| Task 4: Making Predictions | Preparation Time: **30 seconds** | Recording Time: **60 seconds** |

I'll predict what some of the people in this airport scene might do next and some of the things that might happen next. ← In the introduction, briefly describe the scene again. Then state that you will predict what might happen next or what the people might do.

I suspect that the young couple with backpacks will keep talking to each other for a while. I think that the daughter of the couple will soon feel hungry, so her parents will take her to get a snack. I think that the elderly people will feel tired and sit down. I think some of the people sitting on chairs in the background will board their plane. I feel that the man watching the airplane take off will probably stay where he is and watch other planes take off. ← In the body section, mention the things and people in the same order that you mentioned them in Task 3. For each thing or person, try to make a plausible, or likely, prediction about what might happen or what people might do. If you have time, also give a reason why you think so.

Obviously I cannot be sure any of these predictions will come true, but perhaps some of them will. ← In the conclusion, state that you cannot be sure that your predictions will come true but that you think some of them might do so.

This model response has excellent coherence and meaning, good lexical range, high comprehensibility, and great task fulfillment. **If you could deliver a response like this with clear pronunciation and natural rhythm and intonation, you would probably score 11 – 12.**

Task 4 – Practice 4.1

> *Read these three responses to a Task 4 topic. Which response, A, B, or C, is the best one? Why? When you have decided, check your answers on page 109.*

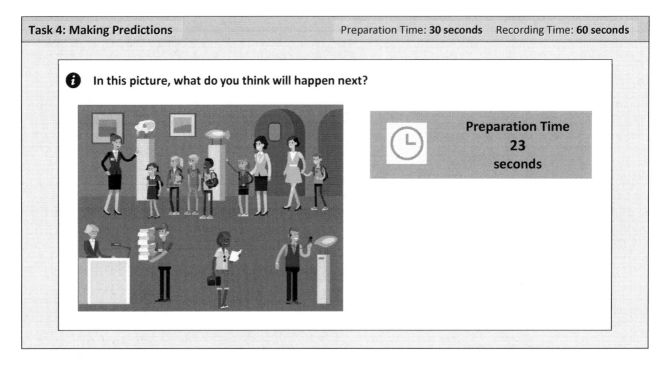

(If you want to see the details of the picture better, remember that the Picture Appendix, which starts on page 118, has a larger version not just of this picture, but of all of the pictures in this Task 4 section.)

Response A

I'll suggest what some of the people in this museum scene might do next and some things that might happen next.

The woman behind her desk might stand up or say something to the man delivering books or boxes. The boy with his mother might walk to another part of the museum. The woman looking at a guide book or map might put it in her pocket or her bag and then go to another part of the museum. The museum guide might answer the schoolgirl's question. The delivery man might put the books or boxes on the desk near the woman. The schoolchildren might ask more questions or look at the exhibits. The man looking at a piece of art and listening to something might take off his headphones.

Obviously I cannot be sure any of my predictions will come true, but perhaps some of them will.

Response B

I'll predict what some of the people in this museum scene might do next and some of the things that might happen next.

I suspect that the museum guide will answer any questions the schoolchildren have and then guide them to another display or exhibit in the museum. I feel that the mother and her son will look at the skull that the schoolchildren were just looking at. I think the delivery person will probably put the books he is carrying on the woman's desk and ask her to sign for them. I imagine that the woman looking at the map will decide where she wants to go. Finally, I think the man looking at the art and listening to something is likely to move on to look at another exhibit.

Obviously I cannot be sure any of these predictions will come true, but perhaps some of them will.

Response C

It's hard to predict what some of the people in this museum scene might do next and some things that might happen next, but here's what I think.

The museum guide will probably continue talking. The schoolchildren will probably continue listening to her. The mother and her son will probably continue walking. The delivery person will probably continue carrying the books or boxes. The woman behind the desk will probably continue sitting. The woman looking at the map or guidebook will probably continue looking at it. The man looking at some art and listening to a recording will probably continue looking at it and listening. Some new visitors will probably enter the museum. That's it.

Obviously I cannot be sure any of these predictions will come true, but perhaps some of them will.

▶ **Now practice the best response until you can say it naturally and fluently in 60 seconds or less.**

Task 4 – Practice 4.2

This response to a Task 4 topic has some missing phrases. Choose the phrase from the list that best completes each blank and write it in the space. Then check the completed response on page 110.

Task 4: Making Predictions	Preparation Time: **30 seconds** Recording Time: **60 seconds**

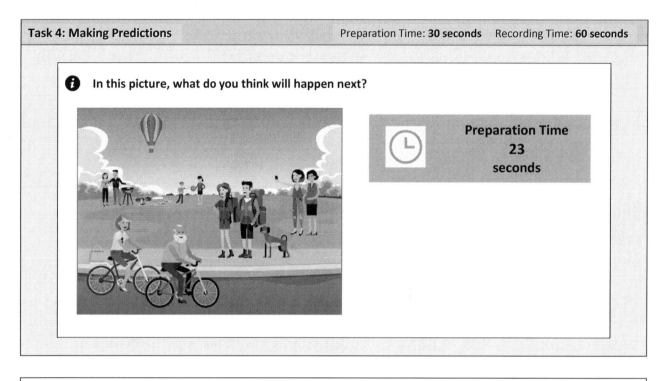

In this picture, what do you think will happen next?

Preparation Time
23
seconds

I'll predict what **1** _____ *in this park scene might do next and some of the things that might happen next.*

I suspect that the two elderly people will continue cycling **2** _____ *in the direction they* **3** _____ *. I feel that the young couple who are wearing backpacks will let their dog* **4** _____ *the park* **5** _____ *get some exercise. The two women taking a selfie will probably take several pictures before* **6** _____ *to decide which selfie is the best one they took. I feel that the parents of the two children who are playing with a ball will say that lunch is ready and then* **7** _____ *will probably have a picnic on the grass. Finally, I feel that the hot air balloon will float off to the east.*

Obviously **8** _____ *any of these predictions will come true, but perhaps some of them will.*

Phrases

are currently heading	I cannot be sure	looking at their phone	some of the people
down the street	in order to	run around in	the whole family

▶ **Now practice the completed response until you can say it naturally and fluently in 60 seconds or less.**

       Test Expert Speaking Practice *for* **CELPIP**®

Task 4 – Practice 4.3

> *This response to a Task 4 topic has a number of grammar and vocabulary mistakes. A test expert has crossed out the errors. Write in the corrections. Then check the corrected response on page 110.*

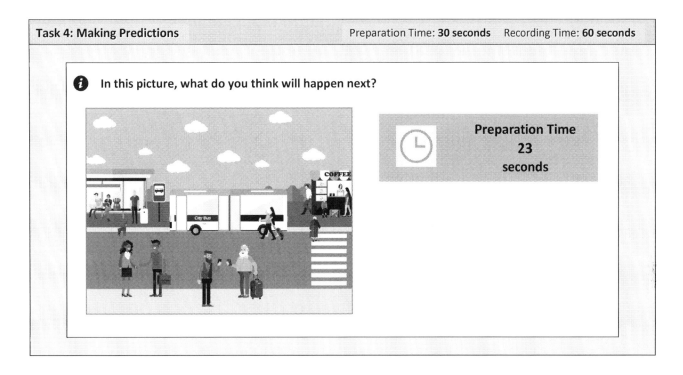

Task 4: Making Predictions	Preparation Time: **30 seconds** Recording Time: **60 seconds**

ℹ In this picture, what do you think will happen next?

Preparation Time
23
seconds

I'll predict what some of the people in this bus station scene might do next and some of the things that might happen next.

I suspect that the people ~~who waiting~~ **1**_____ *in the bus shelter will* ~~pick~~

2_____ *their bags and get on a bus that* ~~take~~ **3**_____ *them to their destination. I feel that the people walking on the road by the bus will either board a bus* ~~and~~

4_____ *move onto the sidewalk. At the café, the woman will finish ordering her coffee and then probably sit down and start* ~~to drinking~~ **5**_____ *it. I imagine that the people shaking hands will go and get a coffee together so they can chat with each other* ~~much easily~~

6_____ *. I think the two men with beards might decide to use their phones* ~~order to~~

7_____ *make a call or perhaps even take* ~~the~~ **8**_____ *photo.*

Obviously I cannot be sure any of these predictions will come true, but perhaps some of them will.

▶ **Now practice the corrected response until you can say it naturally and fluently in 60 seconds or less.**

Task 4 – Practice 4.4

Write your own response to this Task 4 topic using the responses on the previous pages as a guide. After you finish writing your response, compare it with the suggested response on page 110.

Now practice your response until you can say it naturally and fluently in 60 seconds or less.

Task 4 – Practice 4.5

> *Prepare and deliver a response to this Task 4 topic under test conditions. Record your response, if possible. Then listen critically to the recording. Make a list of ways you could improve your response.*

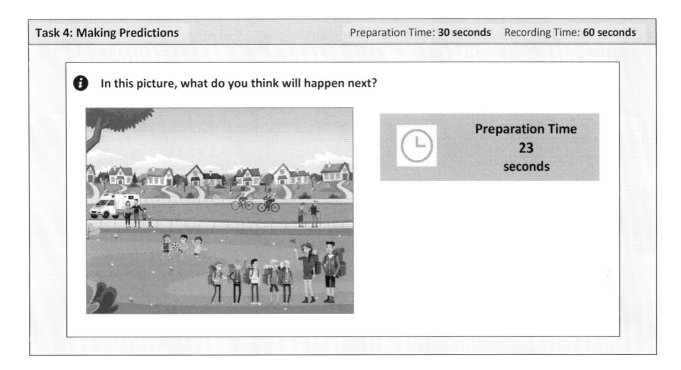

Task 4: Making Predictions	Preparation Time: **30 seconds**	Recording Time: **60 seconds**

ℹ️ **In this picture, what do you think will happen next?**

**Preparation Time
23
seconds**

(If you want to see the details of the picture better, remember that the Picture Appendix, which starts on page 118, has a larger version not just of this picture, but of all of the pictures in this Task 4 section.)

SPEAKING TASK 5

Task 5 – Introduction

After Task 4, the computer will automatically move on to the next question. Task 5 questions ask you to compare two things or places and say which one is better and why. Task 5 has two parts. In the first part, you will have 60 seconds to read about and choose between two things or places. You do not need to speak in this part. In the second part, you will have 60 seconds to prepare reasons why your choice from the first part is better than another person's choice, and 60 seconds in which to deliver your response.

In most cases, the topic will ask you to choose between two household objects, such as two refrigerators, two pieces of office equipment, such as two computers, or two places, such as two holiday destinations. Your main task in the second part of the task is to say why the choice you made is better than the choice that another person made. As with every speaking task, there is no right answer or preferred response.

During the **preparation time** for the first part of Task 5, the computer screen will look something like this:

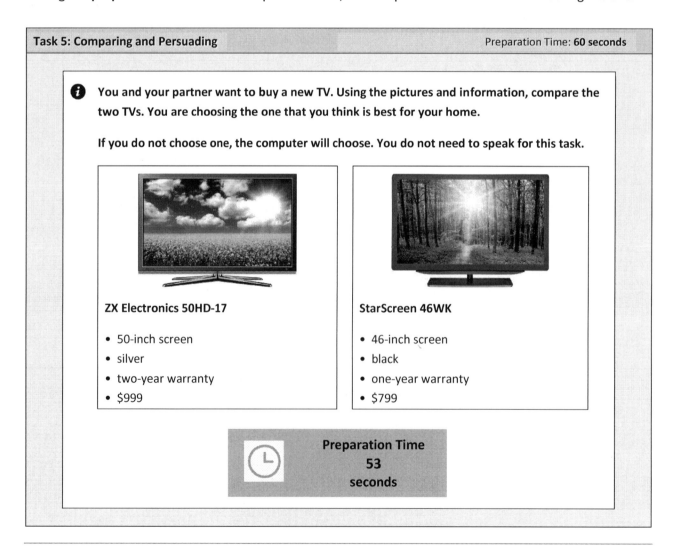

| Task 5: Comparing and Persuading | Preparation Time: **60 seconds** |

> *i* **You and your partner want to buy a new TV. Using the pictures and information, compare the two TVs. You are choosing the one that you think is best for your home.**
>
> **If you do not choose one, the computer will choose. You do not need to speak for this task.**

ZX Electronics 50HD-17

- 50-inch screen
- silver
- two-year warranty
- $999

StarScreen 46WK

- 46-inch screen
- black
- one-year warranty
- $799

Preparation Time
53
seconds

At the top of the screen, you will see the title bar, which shows the speaking task you are currently doing, how much time you have to prepare, and how much time you have in which to speak.

In the middle of the screen, you will see information about the situation. You will also see photographs of the two things you need to choose between. Below each photograph, you will see three to five details about it. Read these details carefully because they will help you decide which option you prefer, and why.

You will also see a timer. This will count down until there is no more preparation time remaining. During the preparation time you do not need to speak, but you *do* need to click on the option you choose. If you do not click on either of the options before the time is up, the computer will randomly choose one of them for you.

After the first part of the task, the computer will automatically go on to the second part of the task:

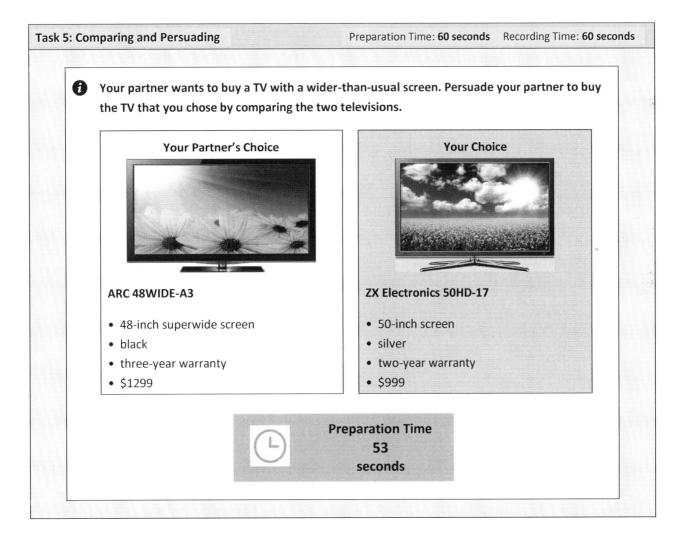

You will see an updated situation and two photographs. The left photo will be a choice made by somebody else, such as your boss, partner, or friend. The right picture will be your choice from the first part. The two choices will be labelled, and your choice will have a different coloured background.

During the second preparation period, you should look at the choice that is indicated as the choice made by the other person and compare it with your choice. Try to think of ways you could persuade the other person that your choice is better.

After the preparation time, the computer will automatically go on to the recording screen:

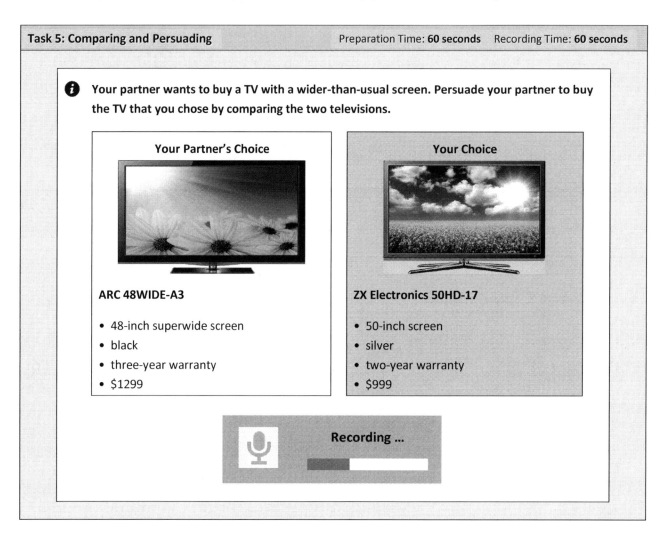

Below the two pictures, you will see an icon of a microphone and a bar showing the time remaining. As soon as you see this screen, you should begin speaking. The computer will automatically record what you say.

After the recording time is up, the computer will stop recording and save your response automatically. You do not need to click anything to save the response. The grey bar will change and look similar to this:

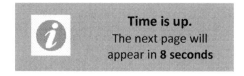

After a few seconds, the computer will automatically go on to Task 6.

Test Expert Speaking Practice *for* **CELPIP**®

Task 5 – How to Organize Your Response

Every Task 5 topic asks you to compare two options – one that you chose in the first part of the task, and one that another person chose. Each question asks you to compare different things, but the questions tend to follow a standard pattern. As a result, you can use the same basic organization for every response.

In general, a good response to a Task 5 question will have the following organization and include the following information.

Introduction	• Say that there are some good things about the other person's choice • Say that you think there are several reasons why your choice is better
Body of Speech	• Give at least two reasons why you think your choice is the better one; as with other speaking tasks in CELPIP, it is important that you support your reasons with details and/or examples
Conclusion	• Express the hope that the other person agrees with your point of view

During the body of your speech, there are two main ways you can give reasons and support for your choice. You can use either or both of these reasons in your response:

- **Explain why your choice is better**

One option is to give a reason why your choice is better than the other choice. This reason will usually come from the details below the photograph, but if you see something in the photograph that you want to talk about, this is also OK.

So, for example, if the Task 5 questions ask you to choose between two televisions, you might say that your choice is better because it has a bigger screen, or a cheaper price, or a better design. You should then follow up with a reason why this is important. For example, you might say that a bigger screen is useful because you will put the TV in a large room, or that a cheaper price is good because you do not have much money right now, or that you like the design because it will look good with the other items in your home.

- **Explain why the other choice is worse**

You could also say why you think the other choice is worse than your choice. Again, the point you make can come from the details below the photograph or from something you see in the photo.

So, for example, you might say that the other choice is not as good because it is black or because it has a particular type of screen. Again, you should follow up each point with a reason why you think it is important. For instance, you might say that a black TV would not look good in your home because your other furniture is white or silver, or that a "superwide" screen is not ideal because most TV shows are not shown in a superwide format.

Task 5 – Step-By-Step Guide

Following these five steps will help you deliver great responses to Task 5 questions.

BEFORE YOU SPEAK

STEP 1   During the 60 seconds of preparation time in the first part of the task, decide which of the two options you will choose, and why. Focus on coming up with reasons that you can explain clearly and easily. Make notes if you wish.

Note: Do not forget to select your preferred option by clicking on it; otherwise, the computer will automatically choose one of the two options but it may not choose the option you prefer.

STEP 2   During the 60 seconds of preparation time in the second part of the task, think how you can say that your choice is better than the other person's choice. Make notes if you wish.

WHILE YOU SPEAK

STEP 3   When the recording time begins, deliver your response. Try to speak clearly and avoid speaking either too quickly or too slowly. Pause briefly after each sentence, but try to avoid long pauses or hesitations in the middle of your sentences because these might reduce your score. Follow your notes, if you have them, so that you remember what you want to say and in what order.

When you are speaking, keep an eye on how much time is remaining. If you see that you are running out of time, start speaking slightly more quickly.

STEP 4   After you have finished your response, check how much time is remaining.

If there is a lot of time left, you can fill the remaining time by saying something that matches the picture, such as "Of course, I'm sure you have good reasons for thinking that your choice is the better option, and I'd be happy to hear them."

If there is little time remaining, it is usually best just to be silent and *not* say anything else.

AFTER YOU SPEAK

STEP 5   Use the time before the next task begins first to take a deep breath. This will help you relax. Then think about what you will need to do in the next task. This will help you prepare more quickly and be ready to use the preparation time as effectively as possible.

Task 5 – Common Mistakes

Some common mistakes that test-takers make in Task 5 include the following:

Not Giving Specific, Relevant Reasons

When you say why you prefer your choice, you need to use specific reasons, details, and examples to explain why it is your preference. If you do not do this, your score may be affected.

★ To avoid this problem, take reasons, details, and examples from the information shown on screen. For example, if you want to say why you think X is good and the information on screen showed that the price of X is relatively cheap at just $50, you could say something like "X is only $50, which is great value" or "X is half the price of Y, which is good because we don't have much money now."

Stating Unsupported Opinions Too Strongly

In Task 5, your goal is to persuade the other person that your choice is better than his or her choice. To do this, it is necessary to express your opinion and support your opinion, but also to show that you understand that the other person's opinion has some merits. If you only focus on your opinion, the raters may feel that you have not fully addressed the task.

★ To avoid this problem, include a statement in your introduction that mentions some advantages or benefits of the other person's choice. In addition, you can mention one or two positive aspects of the other person's choice in the body of your speech.

Task 5 – Useful Language

There are many things you might need to say in a response to a Task 5 question. Here are some functions with example expressions that are likely to be useful:

Introducing two or more reasons or points	• For one thing, … / For another thing, … / For a final thing, … • First (of all), … / Second(ly), … / In addition, … / Finally, …
Comparing two things	• X is much / far/ slightly / a little / bigger / smaller / cheaper / better than … • X is better than Y / X is a better choice than Y / X is not as good as Y
Expressing contrasts	• Even though / though X is … • X is … , but Y is … • In spite of / Despite X being … • X is … ; however, Y is …
Asking for agreement from the other person	• …, don't you think? • I'm sure you (would) agree that … • …, don't you agree? • Wouldn't you say that … ?

Task 5 – Sample Response with Analysis

Read the prompt and the model response by a test expert. Then read the analysis of the response. This will help you understand how to give effective, high-scoring responses to Task 5 questions.

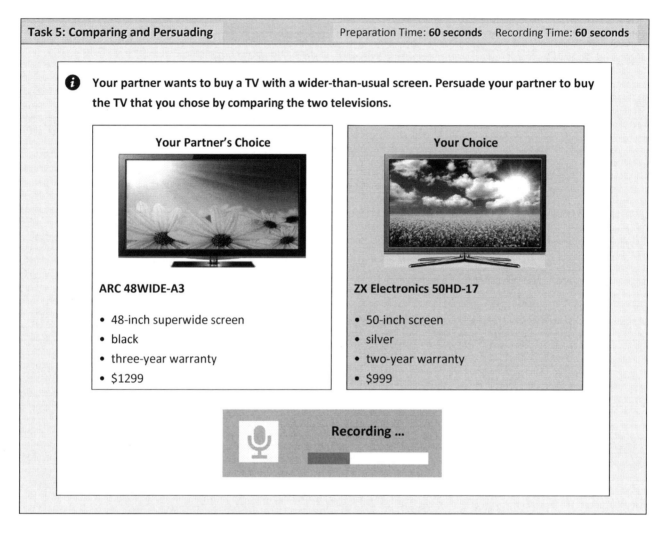

Task 5: Comparing and Persuading Preparation Time: **60 seconds** Recording Time: **60 seconds**

Your partner wants to buy a TV with a wider-than-usual screen. Persuade your partner to buy the TV that you chose by comparing the two televisions.

Your Partner's Choice

ARC 48WIDE-A3

- 48-inch superwide screen
- black
- three-year warranty
- $1299

Your Choice

ZX Electronics 50HD-17

- 50-inch screen
- silver
- two-year warranty
- $999

Recording ...

Note that the details of the photographs in Task 5 questions are not as important as the details of the images in Task 3, Task 4, and Task 8 questions. For this reason, larger versions of the pictures in this Task 5 section are *not* included in the Picture Appendix.

The TV you chose definitely has some good points. ← In the introduction, say that the other's person's
However, there are a couple of reasons why I think choice has some benefits. Then say that there are
my choice is the better option for our home. several reasons why you prefer your choice.

For one thing, the TV made by ZX Electronics is In this case, notice how the speaker mentions
$300 cheaper than the ARC TV. As you know, "our home." This nicely connects his response to
we don't have a lot of money to spend right now, the situation described in the question.
so I think getting a cheaper TV is a better option,
especially as the screen is a little bigger. In the body section, give at least two reasons why
you think your choice is the better one. Be as
For another thing, our DVD player and CD player specific as possible, and support your preference
are both silver, so I think that a silver TV would with relevant ideas. These can be related to the
look better in our home than one which is black. I information on screen or imaginary reasons.
do like the longer warranty that the ARC TV has,
but I really think the silver one is better for us. In this case, notice how the speaker refers to the
financial status of himself and his partner as well
I hope you understand and agree with my reasons as the colour of other things in their home. Both
for thinking that the TV made by ZX Electronics is a of these are relevant (but imaginary) reasons.
better option.
To conclude, sum up your preference and express
the hope that the other person understands.

This model response has excellent coherence and meaning, good lexical range, high comprehensibility, and great task fulfillment. **If you could deliver a response like this with clear pronunciation and natural rhythm and intonation, you would probably score 11 – 12.**

Task 5 – Practice 5.1

Read these two responses to a Task 5 topic. Which response, A or B, is the better one? Why? When you have decided, check your answers on page 110.

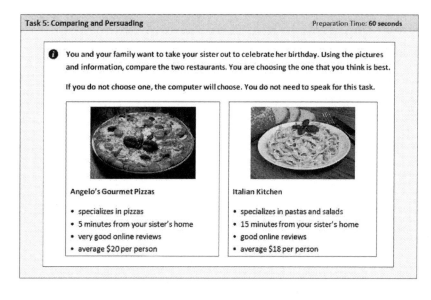

Task 5: Comparing and Persuading   Preparation Time: **60 seconds**

ℹ You and your family want to take your sister out to celebrate her birthday. Using the pictures and information, compare the two restaurants. You are choosing the one that you think is best.

If you do not choose one, the computer will choose. You do not need to speak for this task.

Angelo's Gourmet Pizzas

- specializes in pizzas
- 5 minutes from your sister's home
- very good online reviews
- average $20 per person

Italian Kitchen

- specializes in pastas and salads
- 15 minutes from your sister's home
- good online reviews
- average $18 per person

Second part

Task 5: Comparing and Persuading   Preparation Time: **60 seconds**   Recording Time: **60 seconds**

ℹ Your brother suggests taking your sister to a restaurant that he knows. Persuade your brother to accept your choice by comparing the two restaurants.

Your Brother's Choice

Fruits of the Sea

- specializes in fresh fish and seafood
- 35 minutes from your sister's home
- very good online reviews
- average $45 per person

Your Choice

Italian Kitchen

- specializes in pastas and salads
- 15 minutes from your sister's home
- good online reviews
- average $18 per person

 Preparation Time
53
seconds

Response A

> *The restaurant you chose definitely has some good points, especially because everybody in the family likes fresh fish and seafood. However, it's Mary's birthday, so I think it would be a good idea to ask her where she would like to go.*
>
> *First of all, although I think she would probably enjoy eating at Italian Kitchen, she may feel that she wants to go somewhere more expensive. If so, then Fruits of the Sea might be a very good option, I think.*
>
> *Moreover, she might have eaten either Italian food or fish recently. If so, she would probably prefer to eat out at a different kind of restaurant on her birthday, don't you think? I mean, most people wouldn't want to eat the same kind of food two or three days in a row.*
>
> *I hope you understand and agree with my reasons for suggesting that we should ask Mary her opinion about where to go and what to eat.*

Response B

> *The restaurant you chose definitely has some good points. However, there are a couple of reasons why I think my choice is the better option for Mary's birthday dinner.*
>
> *For one thing, maybe you don't know this, but Mary has recently discovered that she is allergic to some kinds of seafood. Obviously she could avoid ordering these foods, but I'm sure you agree it would be better for her to eat at a restaurant where there is less safety risk.*
>
> *For another thing, the Italian Kitchen is approximately three times cheaper per person than Fruits of the Sea. As you know, I don't have a lot of money to spend right now, so even though it's Mary's birthday, going out to a cheaper restaurant is a better option for me, especially as we know she loves Italian food.*
>
> *I hope you understand and agree with my reasons for thinking that Italian Kitchen is a better option.*

▶ **Now practice the better response until you can say it naturally and fluently in 60 seconds or less.**

Task 5 – Practice 5.2

> *This response to a Task 5 topic has some missing phrases. Choose the phrase from the list that best completes each blank and write it in the space. Then check the completed response on page 111.*

Task 5: Comparing and Persuading   Preparation Time: **60 seconds**

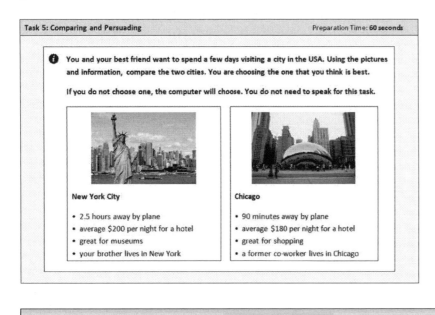

i You and your best friend want to spend a few days visiting a city in the USA. Using the pictures and information, compare the two cities. You are choosing the one that you think is best.

If you do not choose one, the computer will choose. You do not need to speak for this task.

New York City

- 2.5 hours away by plane
- average $200 per night for a hotel
- great for museums
- your brother lives in New York

Chicago

- 90 minutes away by plane
- average $180 per night for a hotel
- great for shopping
- a former co-worker lives in Chicago

Second part

Task 5: Comparing and Persuading   Preparation Time: **60 seconds**   Recording Time: **60 seconds**

i Your best friend wants the two of you to visit Boston for a few days. Persuade your friend to visit the place you chose by comparing the two cities.

Your Best Friend's Choice	**Your Choice**

Boston	**New York City**

Boston

- 2 hours away by plane
- average $160 per night for a hotel
- great for sports and restaurants
- your best friend's uncle lives in Boston

New York City

- 2.5 hours away by plane
- average $200 per night for a hotel
- great for museums and theatres
- your brother lives in New York

 Preparation Time
53
seconds

---

*The city you chose definitely has **1**_____. However, there are a couple of reasons why I think my choice is the better option for our visit to the USA.*

*For one thing, I didn't **2**_____, but my boss has asked me to go to Boston to attend a conference next month. Moreover, **3**_____in Boston several years ago on business. **4**_____you can understand, I **5**_____somewhere I've never been before, which is why New York is my preference.*

*For another thing, a couple of days ago you and I talked about **6**_____on our trip. **7**_____going to museums and the theatre would be great. I know that Boston has museums and theatres, too, but New York is **8**_____for these kinds of cultural attractions.*

I hope you understand and agree with my reasons for thinking that we'd have a better time in New York.

Phrases

as I'm sure that	*much more famous*	*tell you this yet*	*what we want to do*
I spent a few days	*some good points*	*we both agreed that*	*would rather go*

▶ **Now practice the completed response until you can say it naturally and fluently in 60 seconds or less.**

Task 5 – Practice 5.3

This response to a Task 5 topic has a number of grammar and vocabulary mistakes. A test expert has crossed out the errors. Write in the corrections. Then check the corrected response on page 111.

Task 5: Comparing and Persuading   Preparation Time: **60 seconds**

You and your roommate need to get a new sofa for the home you share. Using the pictures and information, compare the two sofas. You are choosing the one that you think is best.

If you do not choose one, the computer will choose. You do not need to speak for this task.

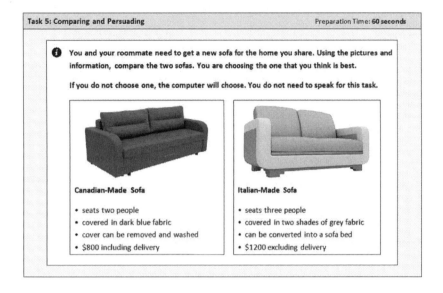

Canadian-Made Sofa

- seats two people
- covered in dark blue fabric
- cover can be removed and washed
- $800 including delivery

Italian-Made Sofa

- seats three people
- covered in two shades of grey fabric
- can be converted into a sofa bed
- $1200 excluding delivery

Second part

Task 5: Comparing and Persuading   Preparation Time: **60 seconds**   Recording Time: **60 seconds**

Your roommate has found a sofa that he likes. Persuade your roommate to accept the sofa that you chose by comparing the two pieces of furniture.

Your Partner's Choice

USA-Made Sofa

- seats two people
- covered in brown leather and fabric
- comes with one-year warranty
- $1250 including delivery

Your Choice

Italian-Made Sofa

- Seats three people
- Covered in two shades of grey fabric
- Can be converted into a sofa bed
- $1200 excluding delivery

Preparation Time
53
seconds

The sofa you ~~choose~~ **1** .... definitely has some good points. However, there are a couple of reasons why I think my choice is the ~~best~~ **2** .... option for our shared home.

First, sometimes we have friends or family members, such as my sister or your brother, come to ~~staying~~ **3** .... at our home, and it would be great to have a sofa bed for a guest ~~could~~ **4** .... sleep on.

Second, ~~but~~ **5** .... I usually like leather sofas, I think the two shades of grey of the Italian-made sofa will look better in our home ~~that~~ **6** .... the brown leather and fabric of your ~~suggestion~~ **7** .... sofa.

Finally, I think it would be good to have a sofa with ~~space enough~~ **8** .... for more than two people. My option is the only sofa with room for three people.

I hope you understand and agree with my reasons for feeling that the Italian-made sofa is a better option.

▶ **Now practice the corrected response until you can say it naturally and fluently in 60 seconds or less.**

Task 5 – Practice 5.4

> *Write your own response to this Task 5 topic using the responses on the previous pages as a guide. After you finish writing your response, compare it with the suggested response on page 111.*

Task 5: Comparing and Persuading	Preparation Time: **60 seconds**

 You are taking a business trip to another city next week. You want to book a hotel to stay in. You are choosing the hotel that you think is best for your needs.

If you do not choose one, the computer will choose. You do not need to speak for this task.

Silver Star Hotel

- built in 2015
- 22 км from the airport
- walking distance to downtown
- $240 per night
- free breakfast

Business Lodge

- built in 1982
- 12 км from the airport
- 2 км from downtown (by subway)
- $185 per night
- free Wi-Fi

**Preparation Time
53
seconds**

 Your manager has said that she thinks you should stay in a hotel she knows. Persuade your manager to accept your choice by comparing the two hotels.

Your Manager's Choice

Airport Traveller Hotel

- built in 1997
- 1 km from the airport
- 19 km from downtown (by car)
- $155 per night
- third night free

Your Choice

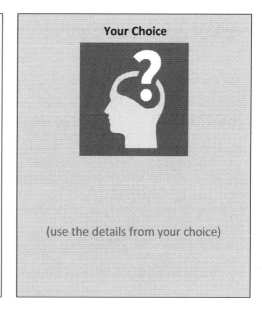

(use the details from your choice)

Recording ...

▶ **Now practice your response until you can say it naturally and fluently in 60 seconds or less.**

Task 5 – Practice 5.5

Prepare and deliver a response to this Task 5 topic under test conditions. Record your response, if possible. Then listen critically to the recording. Make a list of ways you could improve your response.

Task 5: Comparing and Persuading	Preparation Time: **60 seconds**

 You and your business partner need to buy a new laptop computer. Using the pictures and information, compare the two laptops. You are choosing the one that you think is best for your work situation.

If you do not choose one, the computer will choose. You do not need to speak for this task.

Ultralight Convertible Laptop

- 10-inch screen
- black with grey keyboard
- 0.7 KG
- two-year warranty
- $999

Professional Laptop

- 15-inch screen
- black with silver keyboard
- 2.2 KG
- three-year warranty
- $899

 Preparation Time
53
seconds

Your business partner wants to buy an all-purpose laptop. Persuade him or her to buy the one that you chose by comparing the two laptops.

Your Partner's Choice

All-Purpose Laptop

- 13-inch screen
- black with dark silver keyboard
- 1.8 KG
- one-year warranty
- $799

Your Choice

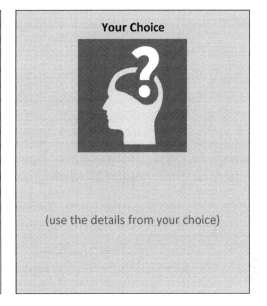

(use the details from your choice)

Recording ...

SPEAKING TASK 6

Task 6 – Introduction

After Task 5, the computer will automatically move on to the next question. Task 6 questions ask you to talk about the reasons why you would choose to do one of two things. The two options are related to a difficult situation that is similar to ones people sometimes experience in their daily lives. **You will have 60 seconds in which to prepare your response, and 60 seconds in which to deliver your response.**

The topic will first give a brief description of a situation. It will then explain what one person, usually a friend or family member, thinks about the situation. Then the topic will give you a choice of two options related to the situation. Each option will require you to speak to a different person.

Your focus in Task 6 should be to give your reasons for choosing one of the two options. You should include persuasive and relevant supporting details or examples. As always, there is no right answer to the topic.

During the **preparation time** for Task 6, the computer screen will look something like this:

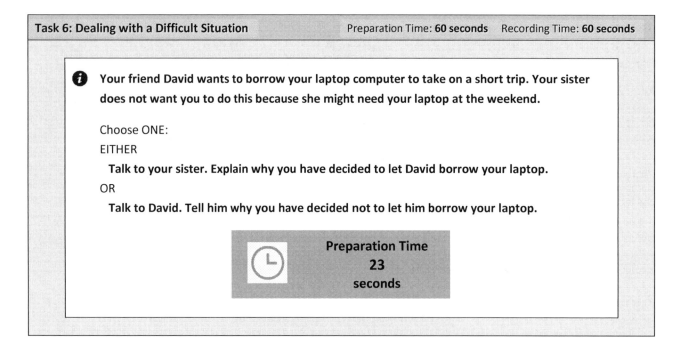

At the top of the screen, you will see the usual title bar showing the speaking task you are currently doing, how much time you have to prepare, and how much time you have in which to speak.

In the middle of the screen, you will see the topic, the situation, and the two options. Below the topic, you will see a timer. This will count down until there is no more preparation time remaining.

Test Expert Speaking Practice *for* **CELPIP**®

After the preparation time is up, the computer will automatically go on to the recording screen:

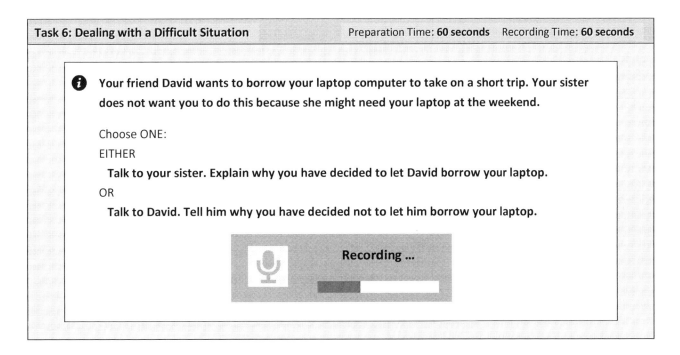

In the middle of the screen you will see an icon of a microphone and a bar showing how much time remains. As soon as you see this screen, begin speaking. The computer will automatically record what you say.

After the recording time is up, the computer will stop recording automatically and the screen will change:

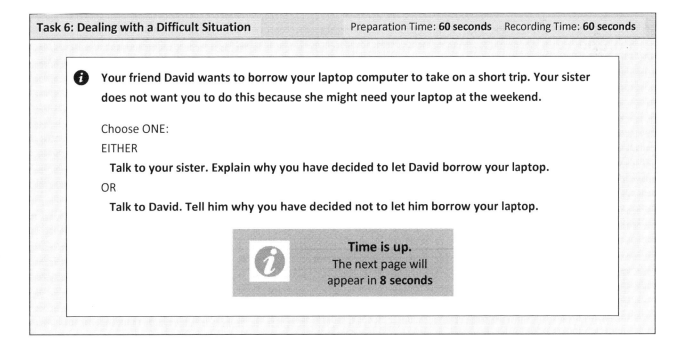

When the computer stops recording, it will automatically save your response. You do not need to click anything to save the response. After a few seconds, the computer will automatically go on to Task 7.

Task 6 – How to Organize Your Response

Every Task 6 topic gives you a different situation and asks you to make a choice between two different options. However, the topics usually follow a standard pattern, so you can use the same basic organization for every response, regardless of the topic.

In general, a good response to a Task 6 question will have the following organization and will include the following information.

Introduction	• Greet the person you are speaking to • Explain the choice you have made and apologize to the person • Mention that you will give your reasons
Body of Speech	• Explain the first reason for your choice • Support your first reason with relevant details and/or examples • Explain the second reason for your choice • Support your second reason with relevant details and/or examples
Conclusion	• Add a concluding statement that summarizes your choice

During the body of your speech, there are two main ways you can give reasons and support for your choice. You can use either or both of these reasons in your response:

- **Focus on negative reasons about one of the choices**

One option is to mention a negative reason or detail about one of the choices. So, for example, if you decide not to let somebody use your laptop, you could say it is because you are worried that this person might lose or damage the laptop.

- **Focus on positive reasons about one of the choices**

Another option is to give positive reasons and details about one of the choices. So, for example, if you decide not to let somebody use your laptop, you could say it is because your sister has a job interview soon and she needs the laptop to prepare for it.

Note that it is possible to give three or even four reasons for your opinion, of course. However, this is not necessary, and in fact, many test-takers find it hard to come up with more than two ideas. As long as you give at least two reasons, you have a good chance to give an effective response and get a good score.

Task 6 – Step-By-Step Guide

Following these five steps will help you deliver great responses to Task 6 questions.

BEFORE YOU SPEAK

STEP 1 Read the topic carefully so that you understand both the situation and what the people mentioned in the topic want you to do. If you make a mistake about a basic detail like this, it is likely to affect your score. As always, make sure that you complete this step as quickly as possible.

STEP 2 Brainstorm reasons why you might choose each option. Also brainstorm details and examples to support each reason. Choose the option you will talk about based on your reasons: the option you should choose is the one with reasons that would be easier for you to talk about.

When brainstorming, you may wish to write down your ideas. You will not have time to write full sentences, so make notes only. You may wish to number your reasons and supporting details in the order you will say them.

WHILE YOU SPEAK

STEP 3 When the recording time begins, deliver your response. Try to speak clearly and avoid speaking either too quickly or too slowly. Pause briefly after each sentence, but try to avoid long pauses or hesitations in the middle of your sentences because these might reduce your score. Follow your notes, if you have them, so that you remember what you want to say and in what order.

When you are speaking, keep an eye on how much time is remaining. If you see that you are running out of time, start speaking slightly more quickly.

STEP 4 After you have finished your response, check how much time is remaining.

If there is a lot of time left, you can fill the remaining time by saying something like "I know this is not what you wanted to hear, but I hope that you understand my choice and my reasons."

If there is little time remaining, it is usually best just to be silent and *not* say anything else.

AFTER YOU SPEAK

STEP 5 Use the time before the next task begins first to take a deep breath. This will help you relax. Then think about what you will need to do in the next task. This will help you prepare more quickly and be ready to use the preparation time as effectively as possible.

Task 6 – Common Mistakes

Some common mistakes that test-takers make in Task 6 include the following:

Giving Unclear, Unconvincing, or Unsupported Reasons

Your main goal in Task 6 is to give reasons for your choice and to support them with specific details and/or examples. If you give reasons that are not clear, not convincing, or not supported, it may affect your score.

★ To avoid this problem, make sure you include clear, obvious reasons for your choice. For example, if you don't want to lend somebody some money, an obvious reason to give would be to say that you do not have much money at the moment. You could then support this point with specific details.

The situation the topic describes may include useful information you can summarize or paraphrase when you give your reasons. For instance, if the situation mentions that the last time you lent this person money, she did not pay it back, this would be a good reason to mention in your response.

Talking in General Terms Rather Than Discussing the Specific Situation

The topic will ask you to choose one of two options related to a specific situation. As a result, it is important to address this specific situation in your response. Talking about the issue in general terms is likely to reduce your score. For example, if the topic is about your laptop, do not discuss laptops or computers in general.

★ To avoid this problem, make sure you use the specific names of the people mentioned in the topic, discuss specific issues mentioned in the prompt, and so on.

Task 6 – Useful Language

There are many things you might need to say in a response to a Task 6 question. Here are some functions with example expressions that are likely to be useful:

Giving a reason	• One reason is that … • This is because …	• Why? Well, … • There are a couple of reasons for …
Saying that you are sorry about something	• I'm sorry, but … • I apologize, but …	• I'm sorry to say that … • Please forgive me, but …
Saying that a decision was hard for you	• This was not an easy choice for me. • It was hard to decide what to do.	• This was a hard choice. • I found it hard to make a decision.
Expressing a cause or effect of something	• … because … • This was caused by …	• As a result, … • In consequence, …

Task 6 – Sample Response with Analysis

Read the prompt and the model response by a test expert. Then read the analysis of the response. This will help you understand how to give effective, high-scoring responses to Task 6 questions.

Task 6: Dealing with a Difficult Situation	Preparation Time: **60 seconds**　Recording Time: **60 seconds**

 Your friend David wants to borrow your laptop computer to take on a short trip. Your sister does not want you to do this because she might need your laptop at the weekend.

Choose ONE:
EITHER
 Talk to your sister. Explain why you have decided to let David borrow your laptop.
OR
 Talk to David. Tell him why you have decided not to let him borrow your laptop.

Hi, David. I've been thinking about whether or not you can borrow my laptop, and I'm sorry to say that I've decided not to lend it to you. There are a couple of reasons for my decision.

In the introduction, state your choice and mention that there are several reasons for it.

In this case, notice how the speaker apologizes to his friend for his decision.

First, my sister might need to borrow my laptop this weekend. She has helped me a lot recently, such as by helping me move into a new apartment. As a result, I feel that I should let her use my laptop if she needs it.

In the body section, give the reasons for your choice. Support them with details or examples.

In this case, notice how the speaker gives specific details to support his preference for letting his sister use his laptop if she needs it. One of them is positive – he wants to give a benefit to his sister – and one of them is negative – he is worried about the loss of his laptop.

Second, I recently read that laptops often get damaged or stolen when people take trips. I really don't want that to happen because my laptop was pretty expensive and I use it regularly.

This was not an easy choice for me, but I don't feel comfortable letting you borrow my laptop. Sorry.

In the conclusion, summarize your choice. You can say that the decision was hard for you and apologize again, if you like, to sound natural.

This model response has excellent coherence and meaning, good lexical range, high comprehensibility, and great task fulfillment. **If you could deliver a response like this with clear pronunciation and natural rhythm and intonation, you would probably score 11 – 12.**

Task 6 – Practice 6.1

Read these two responses to a Task 6 topic. Which response, A or B, is the better one? Why? When you have decided, check your answers on page 112.

Task 6: Dealing with a Difficult Situation	Preparation Time: **60 seconds** Recording Time: **60 seconds**

 You agreed to drive your friend Sam to an interview at 3PM. Now your boss has asked you to attend an important meeting also at 3PM. If you go to the meeting, Sam will miss her interview.

Choose ONE:
EITHER
  Explain to your boss why you cannot attend the meeting.
OR
  Explain to Sam why you cannot drive her to the interview.

Response A

Hi, Sam. I know I promised to drive you to the interview, but I'm sorry to say that my plans have changed and I can't do that anymore. There are two reasons.

First, my boss has asked me to attend a meeting at the same time that I agreed to drive you to the job interview. I've been working on an important project at the office, and I really need to attend this meeting.

Second, I know you said that getting to the interview by car was the only choice, but perhaps you can find a bus or train that stops near the interview location? Or perhaps you could get a taxi or something?

So anyway, I have to attend this meeting. Sorry.

Response B

Hello, Ms Jones. I know you asked me to attend the meeting today at 3 o'clock, but I was hoping you could ask somebody else to attend instead of me. There are a couple of reasons why I say this.

First, I promised my friend Sam that I would drive her to a job interview today at 3 o'clock, and if I do that, obviously I can't attend the meeting. Sam has been having a tough time recently, and I don't want to break my promise to her. I'm sure you can understand.

Second, Peter Smith has been working hard on our project recently, and I think he actually knows more about it than I do. In consequence, I think Peter would be a better person to attend the meeting than me.

I hope you understand my reasons for saying this and can accept my suggestion that Peter should attend.

▶ **Now practice the better response until you can say it naturally and fluently in 60 seconds or less.**

Task 6 – Practice 6.2

This response to a Task 6 topic has some missing phrases. Choose the phrase from the list that best completes each blank and write it in the space. Then check the completed response on page 112.

Task 6: Dealing with a Difficult Situation	Preparation Time: **60 seconds** Recording Time: **60 seconds**

> ⓘ Your friend Maria has invited you to a dinner party at her home on Sunday. Unfortunately, your parents have also asked you to have a family dinner with them on the same day.
>
> Choose ONE:
> EITHER
>   Explain to Maria why you have to decline her invitation.
> OR
>   Explain to your parents why you cannot have dinner with them.

Hi, Mom and Dad. **1** _____ . *Many thanks for the invitation to come round for a family dinner on Sunday.* **2** _____ *that I'm not going to come because I'm going to have dinner with my friend Maria instead. There are* **3** _____ *for my decision.*

First, Maria is going away on a long business trip soon, and this will be **4** _____ *to see her for about six months. I want to* **5** _____ *to chat with her before she goes away. I'm sure that* **6** _____ .

Second, we had a family dinner just a couple of weeks ago, and Thanksgiving is coming up soon, so I think we'll have plenty more opportunities to **7** _____ *in the near future.*

This was not **8** _____ *for me, but I'm sure you can understand and respect my reasons for choosing to have dinner with Maria on Sunday rather than with you.*

Phrases

a couple of reasons	have an opportunity	I'm sorry to say	spend time together
an easy choice	I hope you're well	my last chance	you can understand

▶ **Now practice the completed response until you can say it naturally and fluently in 60 seconds or less.**

Task 6 – Practice 6.3

This response to a Task 6 topic has a number of grammar and vocabulary mistakes. A test expert has crossed out the errors. Write in the corrections. Then check the corrected response on page 112.

Task 6: Dealing with a Difficult Situation	Preparation Time: **60 seconds**	Recording Time: **60 seconds**

> ℹ️ You recently won a free holiday in Hawaii for two people. Both your best friend Michael and your younger brother Brian have asked if they can go with you. Neither of them has had a vacation for several years.
>
> Choose ONE:
> EITHER
>   Talk to your brother. Explain why you have decided to go to Hawaii with Michael.
> OR
>   Talk to Michael. Explain why you have decided to go to Hawaii with your brother.

Hi, Michael. I've been thinking about whether to ~~go~~ **1**_____ Hawaii with you or with

Brian. I'm sorry to say that ~~I'm deciding~~ **2**_____ to go with my brother. There are a

couple of reasons for my ~~choosing~~ **3**_____ .

First, my brother has had a hard time recently. His wife left him, he ~~is being~~ **4**_____ sick,

and then he lost his job. Going to Hawaii with you would be great, but I think ~~of~~ **5**_____

Brian deserves a chance to relax and enjoy himself more.

Second, last time you and ~~me~~ **6**_____ spoke, you seemed worried about your work

situation. I remember you saying that you ~~are~~ **7**_____ working really hard because of

concern that you might lose your job. I am worried that if you take time off now, your boss might decide

you are not serious about your job.

This was not an easy choice for me, but I ~~am hope~~ **8**_____ you understand my reasons

for choosing to go with Brian.

▶ **Now practice the corrected response until you can say it naturally and fluently in 60 seconds or less.**

Test Expert Speaking Practice *for* **CELPIP**®

Task 6 – Practice 6.4

Write your own response to this Task 6 topic using the responses on the previous pages as a guide. After you finish writing your response, compare it with the suggested response on page 113.

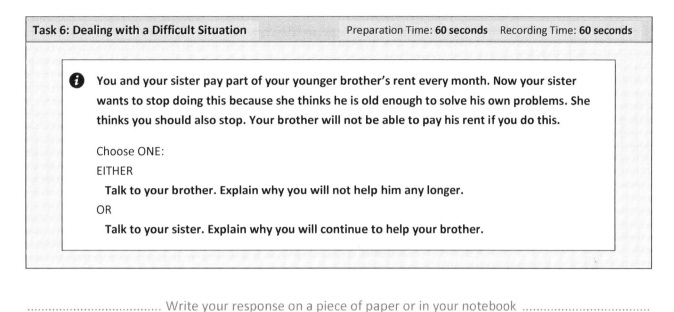

Task 6: Dealing with a Difficult Situation	Preparation Time: **60 seconds** Recording Time: **60 seconds**

i You and your sister pay part of your younger brother's rent every month. Now your sister wants to stop doing this because she thinks he is old enough to solve his own problems. She thinks you should also stop. Your brother will not be able to pay his rent if you do this.

Choose ONE:
EITHER
  Talk to your brother. Explain why you will not help him any longer.
OR
  Talk to your sister. Explain why you will continue to help your brother.

.... Write your response on a piece of paper or in your notebook ....

▶ Now practice your response until you can say it naturally and fluently in 60 seconds or less.

Task 6 – Practice 6.5

Prepare and deliver a response to this Task 6 topic under test conditions. Record your response, if possible. Then listen critically to the recording. Make a list of ways you could improve your response.

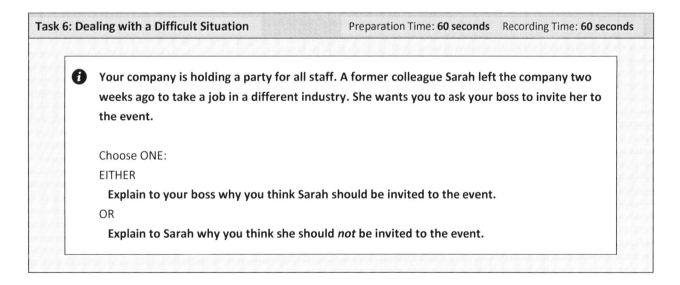

Task 6: Dealing with a Difficult Situation	Preparation Time: **60 seconds** Recording Time: **60 seconds**

i Your company is holding a party for all staff. A former colleague Sarah left the company two weeks ago to take a job in a different industry. She wants you to ask your boss to invite her to the event.

Choose ONE:
EITHER
  Explain to your boss why you think Sarah should be invited to the event.
OR
  Explain to Sarah why you think she should *not* be invited to the event.

SPEAKING TASK 7

Task 7 – Introduction

After Task 6, the computer will automatically move on to the next question. Task 7 questions ask you to express an opinion about a social issue. **You will have 30 seconds in which to prepare your response, and 90 seconds in which to deliver your response.**

The topic will be in two parts: a prompt that tells you to answer the question and give reasons for the views you express, and a yes/no question that asks you about a social issue. The issue will be something that most people are likely to know something about or be able to talk about. The issue will never be controversial or something that might upset people.

Your focus in Task 7 should be to express your opinion clearly, support your point of view with detailed reasons and examples, and organize your response well. As with every speaking task, there is no right answer or preferred response.

During the **preparation time** for Task 7, the computer screen will look something like this:

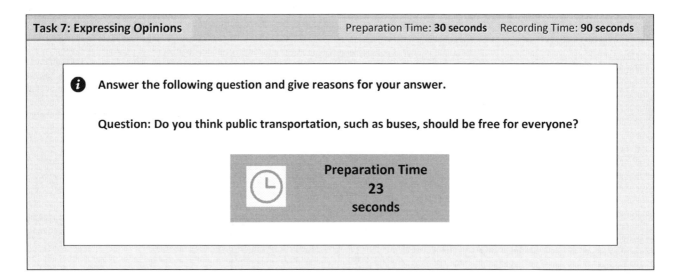

At the top of the screen, you will see the title bar, which shows the speaking task you are currently doing, how much time you have to prepare, and how much time you have in which to speak.

In the middle of the screen, you will see the topic. Below the topic, you will see a timer. This will count down until there is no more preparation time remaining.

After the preparation time has finished, the computer will automatically go on to the recording screen, which will look similar to this:

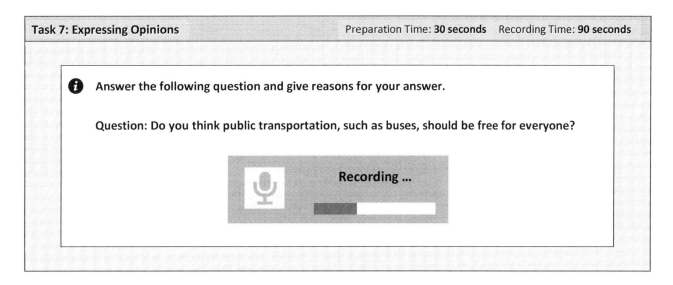

In the middle of the screen you will see an icon of a microphone as well as a bar showing the amount of time remaining in which to record your response. As soon as you see this screen, you should begin speaking. The computer will automatically record what you say. You do not need to click anything to start recording.

After the recording time is up, the computer will stop recording automatically. The screen will change and look similar to this:

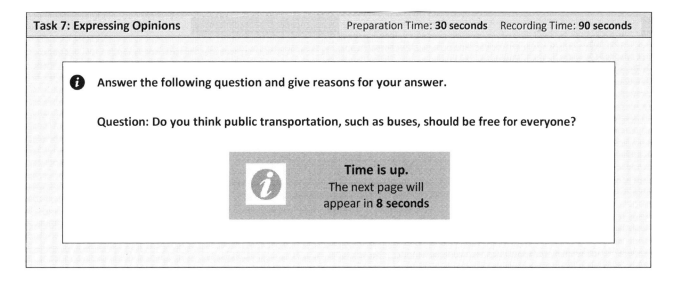

When the computer stops recording, it will automatically save your response. You do not need to click anything to save the response. After a few seconds, the computer will automatically go on to Task 8.

Task 7 – How to Organize Your Response

Every Task 7 topic asks you to talk about a different social issue, but the topics usually follow a standard pattern. As a result, you can generally use one of the following organizations for your response. Often, the choice about how to organize your response depends on the ideas you come up with when brainstorming.

If you came up with two reasons to answer the question in the prompt affirmatively (i.e., saying "yes") or two reasons to answer negatively (i.e., saying "no"), the following organization is a good choice.

Question: Do you think public transportation, such as buses, should be free for everyone?

Introduction	• Say that some people might answer affirmatively (or negatively), but you would answer negatively (or affirmatively)
Body of Speech	• Give one reason with supporting details why you would answer the question negatively (or affirmatively) • Give a second reason with supporting details why you would answer the question negatively (or affirmatively)
Conclusion	• Summarize your answer to the question and express a relevant hope or wish for the future

If you came up with one reason to answer the question affirmatively and one reason to answer it negatively, the following organization is a better choice.

Question: Do you think public transportation, such as buses, should be free for everyone?

Introduction	• Say that the issue is a difficult one and that you can see both sides
Body of Speech	• Give one reason why you would answer the question affirmatively • Give one reason why you would answer the question negatively
Conclusion	• State that if you had to take a position, you would answer affirmatively / negatively

Note that there are many other ways to organize your response, of course. However, the two patterns above are logically organized and natural. Using one of them might help you give an effective response.

Also note that it is possible to give three or even four reasons for your opinion, of course. However, this is not necessary, and in fact, many test-takers find it hard to come up with more than two ideas. As long as you give at least two reasons, you have a good chance to give an effective response and get a good score.

Test Expert Speaking Practice *for* **CELPIP**®

Task 7 – Step-By-Step Guide

Following these five steps will help you deliver great responses to Task 7 questions.

BEFORE YOU SPEAK

STEP 1   Read the topic carefully and understand the limits of the issue. For example, is the issue asking about public transportation *everywhere*, or only *in cities*? If you are not careful about such details, you may talk about the issue too broadly or narrowly, which may affect your score. As always, make sure that you complete this step as quickly as possible.

STEP 2   Brainstorm reasons that match the issue either affirmatively (i.e., saying "yes" to the question in the prompt) or negatively (i.e., saying "no" to the question in the prompt). Make sure you think of reasons that would be easy for you to talk about and easy for the raters to follow. Also brainstorm relevant details or examples you can include to support your reasons.

When brainstorming, you may wish to write down your ideas. You will not have time to write full sentences, so make notes only. You may wish to number your reasons and supporting details in the order you will say them.

WHILE YOU SPEAK

STEP 3   When the recording time begins, deliver your response. Try to speak clearly and avoid speaking either too quickly or too slowly. Pause briefly after each sentence, but try to avoid long pauses or hesitations in the middle of your sentences because these might reduce your score. Follow your notes, if you have them, so that you remember what you want to say and in what order.

When you are speaking, keep an eye on how much time is remaining. If you see that you are running out of time, start speaking slightly more quickly.

STEP 4   After you have finished your response, check how much time is remaining.

If there is a lot of time left, you can fill the remaining time by saying something like "Having said that, I would like to think more about this important issue before making a final decision."

If there is little time remaining, it is usually best just to be silent and *not* say anything else.

AFTER YOU SPEAK

STEP 5   Use the time before the next task begins first to take a deep breath. This will help you relax. Then think about what you will need to do in the next task. This will help you prepare more quickly and be ready to use the preparation time as effectively as possible.

Task 7 – Common Mistakes

Some common mistakes that test-takers make in Task 7 include the following:

Weak Reasons

Although Task 7 is called "Expressing Opinions," in most cases your opinion about the topic is just a "yes" or "no" answer. As a result, it is *not* the most important thing you must discuss. You also need to give relevant, logical, and clear reasons for your opinion. If you do not include such reasons, your score may be affected.

★   To avoid this problem, during the preparation time, focus on coming up with clear, logical reasons for your point of view. Then during the speaking time, make sure you not only express your view, but also give your reasons for holding it.

Unsupported Reasons

A related problem is coming up with reasons that are not supported by details or examples. A great response for Task 7 will include relevant, specific information to support each reason. Responses that include an opinion and reasons but few or irrelevant reasons will probably not get a great score.

★   To avoid this problem, during the preparation time, focus on coming up with supporting details and examples. Then during the speaking time, make sure you not only express your view, but also give reasons for your view, and mention the details and examples that support those reasons.

Task 7 – Useful Language

There are many things you might need to say in a response to a Task 7 question. Here are some functions with example expressions that are likely to be useful:

Expressing your opinion	• I am of the opinion that … • It is my view that …	• In general, I think that … • On the whole, I would say that …
Giving a reason	• The reason is that … • This is because …	• Why? Well, … • The main reason is that …
Giving an example	• For example, … • For instance, …	• such as … • including …
Making general statements about the issue	• I have not really considered this issue before, but … • I'm certainly not an expert on this issue, but … • In my view, this is definitely an important issue, and I would say that … • I can see why some people might think … , but for me …	

Task 7 – Sample Response with Analysis

> *Read the prompt and the model response by a test expert. Then read the analysis of the response. This will help you understand how to give effective, high-scoring responses to Task 7 questions.*

Task 7: Expressing Opinions	Preparation Time: **30 seconds** Recording Time: **90 seconds**

 Answer the following question and give reasons for your answer.

Question: Do you think public transportation, such as buses, should be free for everyone?

I can see why some people might answer this question negatively. In my view, however, there are several reasons why it is my feeling that public transportation should be free.

In the introduction, one option is to begin by saying what other people think about the issue before expressing your own opinion.

For one thing, these days many people are worried about the environment. It is well known that public transportation is better for the environment than private cars because it uses less fossil fuel per person. As a result, in order to reduce pollution levels, I feel the government should make buses, subways, and streetcars free for everyone to use.

In the first body section, give the first reason for your point of view, and support it with details, examples, and so on.

In this case, notice how the speaker connects the issue to another issue (the environment) and uses this as his reason.

For another thing, I read that public transportation is safer than other methods of transportation, especially private cars. If people could use buses and subways for free, more people would probably use them. This would probably result in a reduction in the number of people injured in traffic accidents.

In the second body section, give the second reason for your opinion. As usual, support your reasons with details, examples, and so on.

In this case, notice how the speaker supports his view by referring to the issue of public safety.

To sum up, for the reasons I have given, it is my belief that public transportation should be free for everyone. I hope that this happens sometime in the future, although I think that such a change in the law is rather unlikely.

In the conclusion, summarize your opinion about the issue. Then express a relevant hope or wish.

In this case, notice how the speaker uses natural language to express his hope that public transportation does become free in the future.

This model response has excellent coherence and meaning, good lexical range, high comprehensibility, and great task fulfillment. **If you could deliver a response like this with clear pronunciation and natural rhythm and intonation, you would probably score 11 – 12.**

Task 7 – Practice 7.1

Read these two responses to a Task 7 topic. Which response, A or B, is the better one? Why?
When you have decided, check your answers on page 113.

Task 7: Expressing Opinions	Preparation Time: **30 seconds** Recording Time: **90 seconds**

 Answer the following question and give reasons for your answer.

Question: **Do you think the age at which men and women retire should be raised to 70 years?**

Response A

I can see why some people might agree with raising the age of retirement. In my view, however, there are several reasons why doing this would be a bad idea.

For one thing, a lot of young people are already out of work or unable to find an interesting job with a good salary. If the retirement age is raised, more elderly people will stay in their jobs. I think this will make it even harder for the young to get the job that they want. In my view, this would be bad for society.

For another thing, many jobs these days require employees to be able to use modern technology easily and well. Although some elderly people have this skill, many of them do not. As a result, I feel that if the retirement age is raised, companies may end up with elderly employees who lack the skills that employers need.

To sum up, for the reasons mentioned, I think the retirement age should not be changed. I hope that the government of Canada does not make the decision to raise it in the future.

Response B

This is a difficult question for me to answer because I can see both sides of the issue.

On the one hand, if the retirement age is raised to 70, more elderly people can keep working. This will let them continue to make money and be productive members of society.

On the other hand, some young people will find it hard to get a job because fewer elderly people have retired. This will make it hard for them to make money and be productive members of society.

In conclusion, it is hard to answer this question, but on the whole I think the retirement age should be raised because doing so would allow the elderly to make money and be productive members of society.

▶ **Now practice the better response until you can say it naturally and fluently in 90 seconds or less.**

Test Expert Speaking Practice *for* **CELPIP**®

Task 7 – Practice 7.2

This response to a Task 7 topic has some missing phrases. Choose the phrase from the list that best completes each blank and write it in the space. Then check the completed response on page 113.

Task 7: Expressing Opinions	Preparation Time: **30 seconds** Recording Time: **90 seconds**

> ℹ️ Answer the following question and give reasons for your answer.
>
> Question: Do you think the government should ban advertising for any food that is unhealthy?

I can see why some people might disagree with banning advertisements for unhealthy foods like candy or potato chips. From my **1** _____, however, there are several reasons why doing this would **2** _____ .

3 _____ , more and more young people are suffering from health issues these days. These health issues include diabetes and being overweight. From what I have read and heard, unhealthy food is **4** _____ of these problems, and I think that banning ads for such food would mean that people purchase and eat bad food less often, which might improve the situation.

And second, I think that if companies were only allowed to advertise healthy foods, they would soon change their policies. Currently, many companies produce unhealthy food items, but under the new law, I think they would start developing and advertising healthier foods. These ads **5** _____ to start eating these foods, and this would definitely improve people's health, **6** _____ .

To sum up, for **7** _____ , I think ads for unhealthy foods should definitely be banned. I hope the government decides to do this as **8** _____ .

Phrases

a major cause	first and foremost	may persuade people	soon as possible
be a good idea	in my view	point of view	the reasons given

▶ **Now practice the completed response until you can say it naturally and fluently in 90 seconds or less.**

Task 7 – Practice 7.3

> *This response to a Task 7 topic has a number of grammar and vocabulary mistakes. A test expert has crossed out the errors. Write in the corrections. Then check the corrected response on page 114.*

Task 7: Expressing Opinions	Preparation Time: **30 seconds** Recording Time: **90 seconds**

> ℹ️ Answer the following question and give reasons for your answer.
>
> Question: Do you think children should have to do physical exercise at school every day?

This is a difficult question for me to answer because I can see both sides of ~~issue~~ **1** _____ .

On the one hand, if children were required to do physical exercise ~~everyday~~ **2** _____

at school, I am sure they would be much fitter and healthier. This would be beneficial as they would be sick less often, which would mean their parents wouldn't have to stay ~~in~~ **3** _____ *home to look ~~for~~* **4** _____ *them because they must be absent from school.*

On the other hand, the purpose of school is to educate children. I think teachers should spend their time helping children ~~learning~~ **5** _____ *how to read, how to write, how to calculate, how to solve problems, and so on. If schoolchildren have to spend part of each day running around or doing some kind of sport, obviously they will have ~~fewer~~* **6** _____ *time for serious learning.*

In conclusion, it is hard to answer this question, but on the whole I think that requiring students to play sports or do some ~~another~~ **7** _____ *kind of physical activity is a good idea. I hope that schools in my ~~neighbour~~* **8** _____ *start doing this as soon as possible.*

▶ **Now practice the corrected response until you can say it naturally and fluently in 90 seconds or less.**

Task 7 – Practice 7.4

Write your own response to this Task 7 topic using the responses on the previous pages as a guide. After you finish writing your response, compare it with the suggested response on page 114.

Task 7: Expressing Opinions	Preparation Time: **30 seconds** Recording Time: **90 seconds**

i Answer the following question and give reasons for your answer.

Question: Do you think there should be one public holiday every month in Canada?

....

....

....

....

....

....

....

....

....

▶ Now practice your response until you can say it naturally and fluently in 90 seconds or less.

Task 7 – Practice 7.5

Prepare and deliver a response to this Task 7 topic under test conditions. Record your response, if possible. Then listen critically to the recording. Make a list of ways you could improve your response.

Task 7: Expressing Opinions	Preparation Time: **30 seconds** Recording Time: **90 seconds**

i Answer the following question and give reasons for your answer.

Question: Do you think public transportation, such as buses, should be free for everyone?

SPEAKING TASK 8

Task 8 – Introduction

After Task 7, the computer will automatically move on to the next question. In Task 8, you will see a picture of something unusual. The question will give you a situation and ask you to describe what you can see on the screen to somebody who cannot see it. The question will also give you a second task, such as to ask whether somebody has lost the item shown in the picture or whether it is OK to purchase the item. **You will have 30 seconds in which to prepare your response, and 60 seconds in which to deliver your response.**

Your focus in Task 8 should be to give a description of what you can see. You need to give enough detail that the other person can imagine it. You are unlikely to know the exact words to describe the picture, so you will have to be creative in using the words you *do* know to describe what you can see.

During the **preparation time** for Task 8, the computer screen will look something like this.

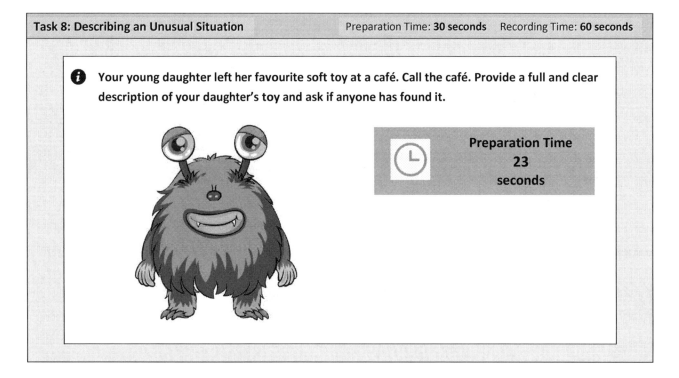

Task 8: Describing an Unusual Situation	Preparation Time: **30 seconds**	Recording Time: **60 seconds**

ⓘ **Your young daughter left her favourite soft toy at a café. Call the café. Provide a full and clear description of your daughter's toy and ask if anyone has found it.**

Preparation Time
23
seconds

At the top of the screen, you will see the title bar, which shows the speaking task you are currently doing, how much time you have to prepare, and how much time you have in which to speak.

In the middle of the screen, you will see the topic and the picture. (Note that you can see a larger version of all the pictures in the Task 8 section in the Picture Appendix, which starts on page 118.) Next to the picture, you will see a clock icon and a timer, which will count down until there is no preparation time left.

Test Expert Speaking Practice *for* **CELPIP**®

After the preparation time, the computer will automatically go on to the recording screen:

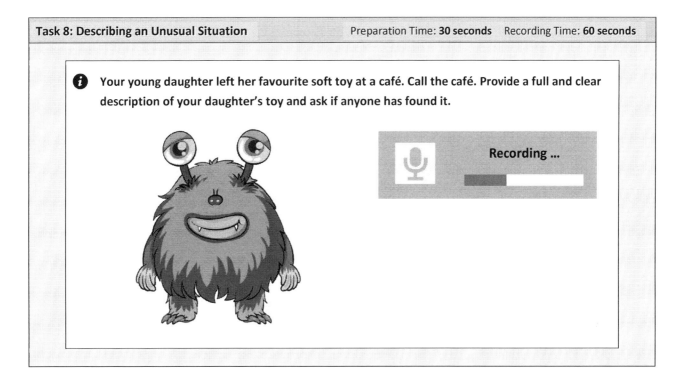

Task 8: Describing an Unusual Situation   Preparation Time: **30 seconds**   Recording Time: **60 seconds**

ⓘ Your young daughter left her favourite soft toy at a café. Call the café. Provide a full and clear description of your daughter's toy and ask if anyone has found it.

Recording ...

Next to the picture, you will see an icon of a microphone and a bar showing the amount of time remaining in which to record your response. As soon as you see this screen, you should begin speaking. The computer will automatically record what you say. You do not need to click anything to start recording.

After the recording time is up, the computer will stop recording and save your response automatically. You do not need to click anything to save the response. The grey bar on the screen will change to look similar to this:

ⓘ   **Time is up.**

Because Task 8 is the last question in the CELPIP Test, after a few seconds the computer will automatically end the test.

Task 8 – How to Organize Your Response

Every Task 8 topic shows you a different picture, but in general the pictures are similar to one another. As a result, you can use the same basic organization for your response provided that you vary the body of your speech depending on what kind of picture you get.

In general, a good response to a Task 8 question will have the following organization and include the following information.

Introduction	• Explain why you are calling by summarizing the situation given in the question • State that you will describe what you can see in the picture
Body of Speech	• Give a brief overall description of the object or thing in the picture (if necessary) • Describe the main features of the picture; include as much detail as possible about each feature you describe; in addition, try to say either where each thing is in relation to the picture (e.g., "on the left …") or where it is in relation to something else in the picture (e.g., next to the …)
Conclusion	• Express the hope that your description was good enough • Ask the question you were told to ask in the Task 8 question topic

In the body of your speech, you should follow a logical order when you describe the main features of the picture. Generally, you should follow one of these three approaches:

• **Describe the Main Features of the Picture from Left to Right**

If the picture is wider than it is tall, usually the best option is first to describe the features you can see on the left of the picture, then what you can see in the middle of the picture, and finally what you can see on the right of the picture.

• **Describe the Main Features of the Picture from Top to Bottom**

If the picture is taller than it is wide, the best option may be to describe the features you can see in the top of the picture, then what you can see in the middle of the picture, and finally what you can see in the bottom of the picture.

Task 8 – Step-By-Step Guide

Following these four steps will help you deliver great responses to Task 8 questions. (Note that because Task 8 questions ask you to describe a picture, you do not need to follow the usual step of carefully reading and understanding the topic.)

BEFORE YOU SPEAK

STEP 1 Look at the whole picture. Decide whether you will describe it from left to right or from top to bottom. Then decide which features of the picture you will describe and how you will describe them. Note that you may not know the names of some of features you could describe. In such cases, you can either think about how to describe the feature using other words, or you can choose to describe other features instead of this feature.

You may find it helpful to draw an outline of the picture and then draw numbers in the same places as the features you will describe. This will help you follow a clear organization. You may also find it helpful to make notes about what you will say during the recording phase.

WHILE YOU SPEAK

STEP 2 When the recording time begins, deliver your response. Try to speak clearly and avoid speaking either too quickly or too slowly. Pause briefly after each sentence, but try to avoid long pauses or hesitations in the middle of your sentences because these might reduce your score. Follow your notes, if you have them, so that you remember what you want to say and in what order.

When you are speaking, keep an eye on how much time is remaining. If you see that you are running out of time, start speaking slightly more quickly.

STEP 3 After you have finished your response, check how much time is remaining.

If there is a lot of time left, you can fill the remaining time by saying something like this as the last sentence of your response: "Of course, if you want me to describe any aspect of <u>the thing</u> again, I'd be happy to do that." (Replace "<u>the thing</u>" with a description of or the name of the object. For example, if you are describing a child's toy, say "Of course, if you want me to describe any aspect of <u>my daughter's toy</u> again, I'd be happy to do that.")

If there is little time remaining, it is usually best just to be silent and *not* say anything else.

AFTER YOU SPEAK

STEP 4 Task 8 is the final task in the CELPIP Test, so relax, take a deep breath, feel proud of yourself, and think of something enjoyable you can do to celebrate having finished the test.

Task 8 – Common Mistakes

Some common mistakes that test-takers make in Task 8 include the following:

Long or Frequent Pauses while Speaking

Because Task 8 asks you to describe something unusual, it is likely that you will not know all of the correct words to describe the picture. This is expected. However, if you hesitate too often or for too long while describing the main features of the picture, your score is likely to be affected.

★ To avoid this problem, you need to describe the main features of the picture using indirect ways to express your points even if you do not know the correct word. For example, if you had to describe the child's toy shown on page 99, you could say something like "It has big round eyes on top of what look like thin sticks." This would clearly describe the picture and impress the raters even though native English speakers would probably say the eyes are on "stalks" instead of "thin sticks."

Incomplete or Short Responses

Because you are unlikely to know the correct words to describe the main features of the picture, you may focus only on the features you know how to describe. This may result in a short, low-scoring response.

★ To avoid this problem, add more details about those features of the picture you are confident you can describe. For example, instead of a short description like "The toy is covered in fur," you could make your response longer by adding more details: "The toy looks like it is covered in hair or fur. The fur appears quite long and seems to be two colours – lighter in some places, darker in other areas."

Task 8 – Useful Language

There are many things you might need to say in a response to a Task 8 question. Here are some functions with example expressions that are likely to be useful:

Describing something using indirect language	• It looks similar to … / like … • It seems as if … / to be … / like …	• It resembles … • It appears to be …
Describing features	• It is made of … / composed of … • It is covered | in / with …	• It is full of … • It has …
Saying where one feature is	• next to … / near … / beside … • above … / level with … / below …	• on the front / back (of) … • on top of … / under …
Admitting that you do not know a word	• I'm not sure exactly what to call it, but … • I don't know if this is the correct name for it, but …	

Task 8 – Sample Response with Analysis

Read the prompt and the model response by a test expert. Then read the analysis of the response. This will help you understand how to give effective, high-scoring responses to Task 8 questions.

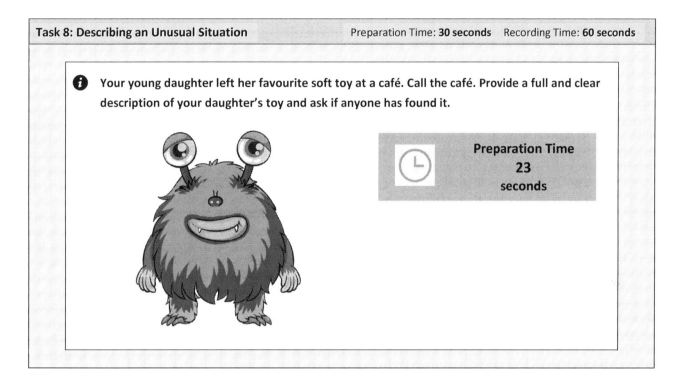

Task 8: Describing an Unusual Situation	Preparation Time: **30 seconds** Recording Time: **60 seconds**

Hello. I'm calling because my child left her favourite toy at your café. Let me describe the toy for you.

The toy is a little alien monster. It has big round eyes on top of what look like thin sticks. Below the eyes it has a small nose that somewhat resembles a pig's nose, and a large curved mouth with two small sharp teeth. It has two arms and two legs. The toes have sharp things that look like knives. The toy looks like it is covered in hair or fur. The fur appears quite long and seems to be two colours – lighter in some places, darker in other areas.

I hope my description of her toy is clear. Do you happen to know if anyone has found it?

In the introduction, summarize or paraphrase the situation given in the topic. Then say that you will describe the thing(s) in the picture.

In the body section, describe the main features of the thing in the picture. Include as many details as possible. Use indirect language if you don't know the exact word for something. (Note that the Task 8 model responses deliberately use indirect language rather than exact words in order to be a more useful model for students.)

In the conclusion, express the hope that your description is clear. Then finish by asking the question that the topic tells you to ask.

This model response has excellent coherence and meaning, good lexical range, high comprehensibility, and great task fulfillment. **If you could deliver a response like this with clear pronunciation and natural rhythm and intonation, you would probably score 11 – 12.**

Task 8 – Practice 8.1

> *Read these three responses to a Task 8 topic. Which response, A, B, or C, is the best one? Why?*
> *When you have decided, check your answers on page 114.*

Task 8: Describing an Unusual Situation	Preparation Time: **30 seconds** Recording Time: **60 seconds**

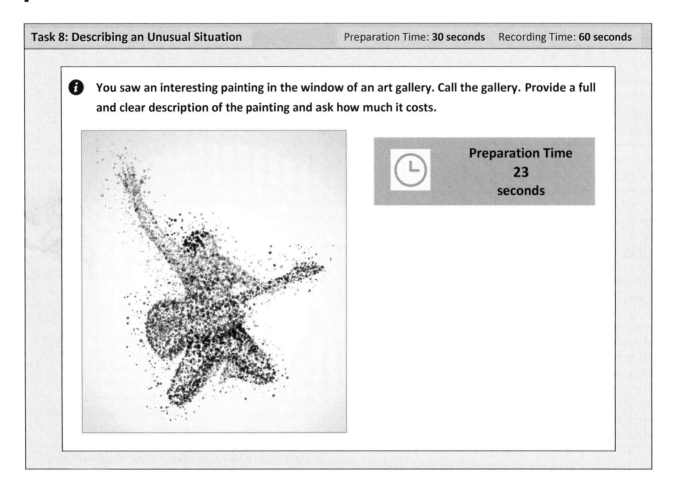

ⓘ You saw an interesting painting in the window of an art gallery. Call the gallery. Provide a full and clear description of the painting and ask how much it costs.

Preparation Time
23
seconds

If you want to see the details of the picture better, remember that the Picture Appendix, which starts on page 118, has a larger version of this picture (and all of the pictures in this Task 8 section).

Response A

Could you tell me about the painting in your window, please? I'd like to buy it, I think.

The painting shows a person playing a guitar. He or she is playing the guitar with one hand. He or she is jumping in the air. He or she has the other hand raised in the air. He or she has both legs up. The guitar looks like an electric guitar. I hope my description of the painting is clear. I think my friend would like the painting because she plays the guitar.

Like I said, the painting is in the window of your art gallery. Please let me know how much the painting costs so that I can think about buying it for my friend.

Response B

Hi. I saw a painting in the window. I'll try to describe it. Do you still have it? How much does it cost?

The painting has many dots. Some of the dots are big and some of them are small. The painting shows a man playing the guitar. It looks like the man's holding the guitar in his left hand. The man is jumping up with his right hand in the air. He's probably having a good time playing at a concert or something. The man is in the middle of the painting. The painting has a thin border around it, which might be a frame or something.

There are more things I could say about the painting, but I just want to know how much it costs.

Response C

Hello. I'm calling about an interesting piece of art that I saw in the window of your gallery a few days ago. I'd like to describe the painting for you.

The painting shows a person playing the guitar. The person appears to be a man and the instrument looks like an electric guitar. It looks as if the man is jumping in the air. His right arm is raised high in the air and his left hand seems to be holding the thin part of the guitar. The most interesting feature of the painting is that the person and his guitar are composed of small and large dots of different shades. There are some dots around the edge of the man, too.

I hope my description of the painting is clear. Do you happen to know how much it costs?

▶ **Now practice the best response until you can say it naturally and fluently in 60 seconds or less.**

Task 8 – Practice 8.2

This response to a Task 8 topic has some missing phrases. Choose the phrase from the list that best completes each blank and write it in the space. Then check the completed response on page 115.

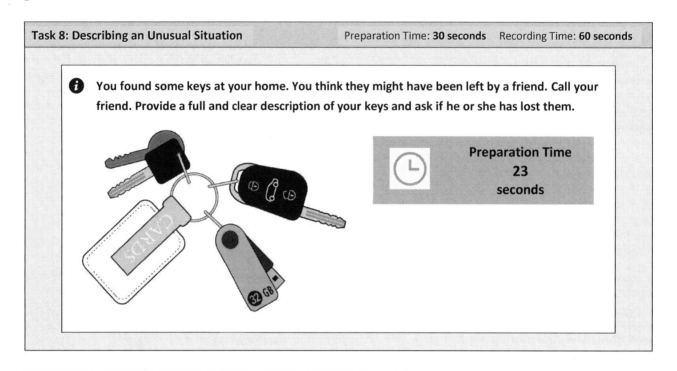

Task 8: Describing an Unusual Situation	Preparation Time: **30 seconds** Recording Time: **60 seconds**

ⓘ You found some keys at your home. You think they might have been left by a friend. Call your friend. Provide a full and clear description of your keys and ask if he or she has lost them.

Preparation Time
23
seconds

Hi. I'm calling because I think there's **1** _____ *by mistake you left your keys*

2 _____ *. I'll describe them for you.*

There's a ring in the middle which has **3** _____ *keys and objects attached to it. One key is a car key. It has a black part with a picture of a car on it* **4** _____ *buttons to lock and unlock the car doors. Next to that is* **5** _____ *some USB memory. It has the number "32" and the letters "GB" on it* **6** _____ *. Next to that is what seems to be a pocket for holding credit cards* **7** _____ *a driver's licence. Finally, there are two keys that are linked together. One looks like it is made of metal. The other* **8** _____ *a square plastic top.*

I hope my description of the keys is clear. Do you think they're yours?

Phrases

a chance that	*appears to have*	*at my place*	*or perhaps a*
a number of	*as well as*	*at the bottom*	*what looks to be*

▶ **Now practice the completed response until you can say it naturally and fluently in 60 seconds or less.**

Test Expert Speaking Practice *for* **CELPIP**®

Task 8 – Practice 8.3

> *This response to a Task 8 topic has a number of grammar and vocabulary mistakes. A test expert has crossed out the errors. Write in the corrections. Then check the corrected response on page 115.*

Task 8: Describing an Unusual Situation	Preparation Time: **30 seconds** Recording Time: **60 seconds**

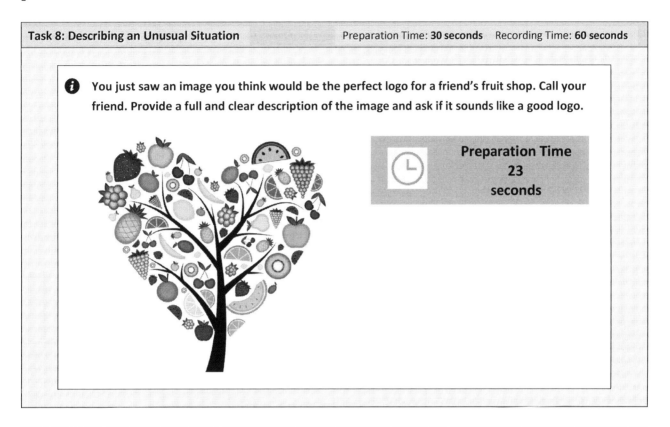

ℹ️ You just saw an image you think would be the perfect logo for a friend's fruit shop. Call your friend. Provide a full and clear description of the image and ask if it sounds like a good logo.

🕐 **Preparation Time 23 seconds**

Hi. I'm calling because I saw an image that might be a great logo for your business. ~~Let me to~~

1 _____ describe it for you.

The image ~~has~~ **2** _____ a tree. The main part of the tree and the branches are black and ~~looks like~~ **3** _____ a normal tree. The leaves of the tree are interesting and different, ~~although~~ **4** _____ . For one thing, the image has different kinds of fruit ~~rather of~~ **5** _____ real leaves. These fruits include strawberries, pineapples, grapes, apples, melons, cherries, oranges, ~~or~~ **6** _____ other varieties. In addition, the fruits suggest good ~~healthy~~ **7** _____ because they are in the shape of a heart.

I hope my description of the image is clear. Do you think that it ~~can~~ **8** _____ be a good logo for your fruit store?

▶ **Now practice the corrected response until you can say it naturally and fluently in 60 seconds or less.**

Task 8 – Practice 8.4

> *Write your own response to this Task 8 topic using the responses on the previous pages as a guide.*
> *After you finish writing your response, compare it with the suggested response on page 115.*

Task 8: Describing an Unusual Situation	Preparation Time: **30 seconds** Recording Time: **60 seconds**

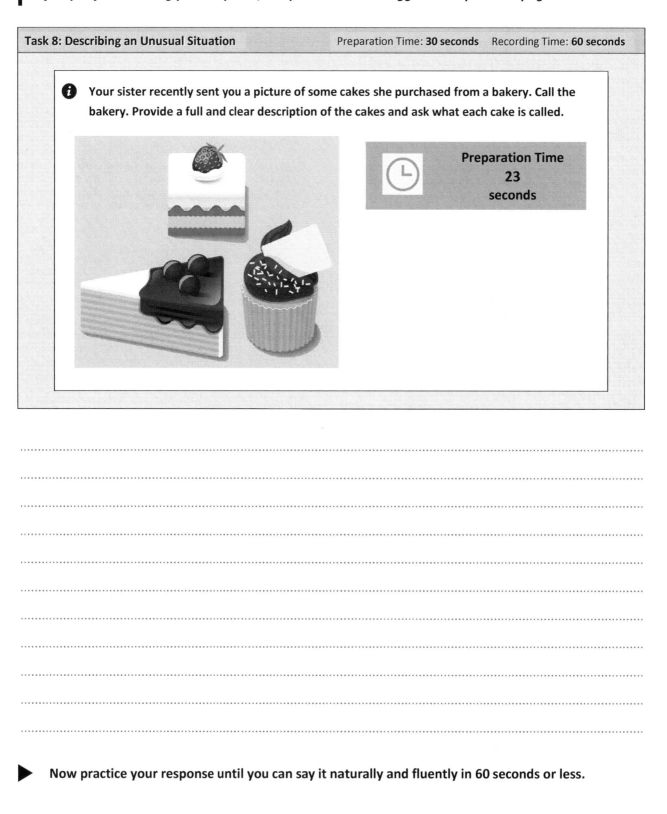

ⓘ Your sister recently sent you a picture of some cakes she purchased from a bakery. Call the bakery. Provide a full and clear description of the cakes and ask what each cake is called.

Preparation Time
23
seconds

....

....

....

....

....

....

....

....

....

....

▶ Now practice your response until you can say it naturally and fluently in 60 seconds or less.

Task 8 – Practice 8.5

> *Prepare and deliver a response to this Task 8 topic under test conditions. Record your response, if possible. Then listen critically to the recording. Make a list of ways you could improve your response.*

Task 8: Describing an Unusual Situation	Preparation Time: **30 seconds** Recording Time: **60 seconds**

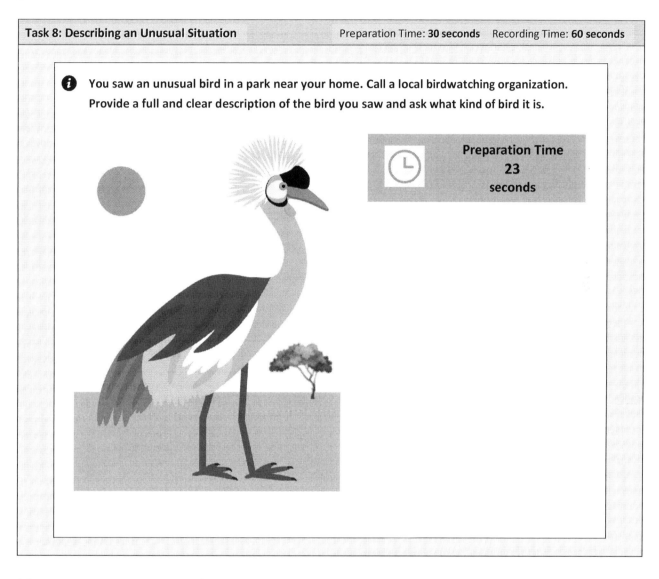

ℹ You saw an unusual bird in a park near your home. Call a local birdwatching organization. Provide a full and clear description of the bird you saw and ask what kind of bird it is.

Preparation Time
23
seconds

(If you want to see the details of the picture better, remember that the Picture Appendix, which starts on page 118, has a larger version not just of this picture, but of all of the pictures in this Task 8 section.)

ANSWERS AND MODEL RESPONSES

Note: if you are not sure why an answer is correct (or incorrect), consult a grammar book or ask a teacher. And remember: you can hear recordings of all of the model responses in this book if you subscribe to the "Test Expert" channel on YouTube.

Practice 1.1 – Explanation

Response B is the better response. The grammar, vocabulary, and language use are all natural and correct. It offers clear reasons why the speaker feels that Canada is a better choice for a vacation than the United States, and gives relevant supporting details and examples. A response like this would probably get a score of 11 to 12.

In contrast, Response A does not address the topic well because it fails to give clear advice about whether the listener should take a vacation in Canada or the USA. In addition, response A is likely to be too short.

Practice 1.2 – Completed Response

Hi, David. I understand that you're thinking about quitting your job and going back to college to study. **As you know**, I did that a few years ago, so perhaps I can give you some advice.

On the one hand, there are definitely some benefits to your plan. **For one thing**, improving your education may help you in the future. Getting an MBA **definitely helped me** find a really great job because employers wanted somebody with an advanced qualification. And for another thing, I know that you really dislike your current position at ABC Industries, so maybe a career change **would be good** for you.

On the other hand, there are some possible drawbacks to your idea. First, the economy may not be in a good state in the future. As a result, **you might find** it hard to get a job after you graduate from college. **And second**, college fees are high right now. This means that you might be in financial trouble if you decide to go back to school.

Anyway, **whatever you decide** to do, I'm sure you'll have a lot of success in the future.

Practice 1.3 – Corrected Response

Hi, Sarah. I understand **you're** interested in becoming healthier. I really tried to improve my health last year, so perhaps I can give you some helpful **advice**.

First, if I were you, I would try to eat healthy food, **especially** fruits and vegetables. I read an interesting article about this topic last year. **According to** what I read, eating plenty of fruits and vegetables can help one lose **weight** and stay healthy. I started trying to eat more healthily last year, and since then, I've lost five kilograms and have hardly been sick at all. Perhaps you'll have the same results as me.

Second, have you considered doing **regular** exercise in the park **near** your home? That park has a running track, a cycle path, and a public swimming pool, so you could do a variety of different types of workouts. The track and path are free, I **believe**, and the pool is inexpensive at just $5 per time, so exercising there wouldn't cost you a lot.

Anyway, whatever you decide to do, good luck! I sincerely hope that you achieve your goal of becoming healthier.

Practice 1.4 – Suggested Response

Hi, David. I understand you're going to move soon. As you know, I moved into a new apartment a few months ago, so perhaps I can give you some helpful suggestions.

First, I strongly suggest that you move into an apartment downtown rather than one on the edge of the city. There are a couple of reasons why I recommend this. First, even though a downtown apartment is more expensive, you will probably save money in the long run. The reason is that you will probably save money on travel expenses every time you go out or commute to your office.

Second, I think your life will be much more enjoyable if you live downtown. When I lived on the edge of the city I often used to feel bored, especially at weekends, because there was almost nothing to do near where I lived. Since I moved into my new apartment downtown, however, I haven't been bored. The reason is that there are so many great things to do and exciting places to go nearby.

Anyway, good luck with your decision. I'm sure you'll make the right choice for you.

Practice 2.1 – Explanation

Response A is the better response. The grammar, vocabulary, and language use are all natural and correct. It clearly describes a mistake the speaker has made, why it was a mistake, and what the speaker learned as a result of making this mistake. A response like this would probably get a score of 11 to 12.

In contrast, Response B does not address the topic well or directly. It describes an argument, but does not directly explain why the speaker thinks the argument was a mistake. In addition, it says how the speaker feels about the experience, but does not say what the speaker learned from it.

Practice 2.2 – Completed Response

In my life, I have had to make difficult choices several times. If I had to pick **just one example** to talk about, however, it would be deciding **whether or not** to help my friend.

A couple of years ago, my friend James was **in financial difficulties**. One month, he needed $1000 to pay his rent, and he asked **if he could** borrow it from me. I really wanted to help him. However, my parents **always told me** not to lend money to friends, so I said no to James. He said that he understood and that **we would still be** friends, but actually we stopped seeing each other **after that**.

To be honest, I miss spending time with James, so I wish that I had loaned him the money he needed.

Practice 2.3 – Corrected Response

In my life, I have had surprising experiences **a number of** times. If I had to pick just one example to talk about, however, it would be winning a scholarship to **go to** a conference.

It happened just **a few** weeks ago. I saw an article online about a conference in Australia. The article **said** that one person could win a scholarship to attend. I've always wanted to **visit** Australia and the conference sounded interesting, so I decided to apply. However, the deadline was in just a few hours, so I had to complete the application extremely **quickly**.

I thought that I had no chance, so I was **both** surprised and pleased when I found out that I had won! Now, however, I'm nervous **because** I have to speak in front of hundreds of people.

Practice 2.4 – Suggested Response

In my life, I have had a great time with my friends many times. If I had to pick just one time to talk about, however, it would be going to Niagara Falls with them.

It happened a few years ago. My friends Jack, Ben, and I had just graduated from university, and we decided to take a trip together to celebrate. Surprisingly, none of us had been to Niagara Falls before, so we took a trip there. We had a wonderful time. We saw the Falls, went to some great restaurants, and met some interesting people.

The whole trip was a great experience, but the best part for me was spending time with Jack and Ben. We had so much fun that every year we go back to Niagara Falls for a couple of days.

Practice 3.1 – Explanation

Response C is the best response. The grammar, vocabulary, and language use are all natural and correct. It uses a logical organization – from top to bottom – and gives a clear description of the people in the scene and where they are or what they are doing. A response like this would probably get a score of 11 to 12.

In contrast, rather than describing the scene and the people in it, the speaker in Response A just gives a list of everything and everybody he can see in the picture. In addition, the response is not well organized. The speaker does not follow a logical order when describing who and what he can see, but "jumps" around. A listener would find it hard to get a mental image of the picture from this response.

Like Response A, Response B is organized poorly. The speaker describes the scene from left to right, but this creates confusion. For example, the speaker mentions there are two women on the left of the picture. This suggests that the women are near each other and/or interacting, but in fact the woman raising her hand and talking and the woman sitting behind a desk are not near each other or interacting in any way. Again, a listener would find it hard to get a clear impression of the picture from this response.

Practice 3.2 – Completed Response

This scene shows **what looks like** a street with a park behind it. I'll describe some of the things and people I can see in the picture **and say what** they're doing.

In the foreground of the picture, two elderly people are riding bicycles. **Just behind them** on the sidewalk are a young couple with a dog. They are wearing backpacks. **In the middle of** the picture I can see two women taking a selfie. **One of them** seems to be pregnant. In the background I can see a family. **It seems as if** they're having a picnic. The parents are cooking some food on a barbecue and their two children are playing with a ball. I can see a hot air balloon **in the sky** behind them.

There is more I could describe, but I hope this gives a clear overall impression **of the scene.**

Practice 3.3 – Corrected Response

This scene **shows** what looks like a bus station or bus stop. I'll **describe** some of the things and people I can see in the picture and say what they're doing.

At the top of **the** picture, there are people waiting in **a** bus shelter. There is a bus near them, and some people walking **on** the road next to the bus. To the right of the bus, there is a café. A woman seems to be ordering a coffee. At the bottom of the picture, a man and a woman **are shaking** hands. Near them I can see two men looking **at** their phones. Both have beards, but one is young and one is older. **The latter** has a small suitcase.

There is more I could describe, but I hope this gives a clear overall impression of the scene.

Practice 3.4 – Suggested Response

This scene shows what looks like a train or subway station. I'll describe some of the things and people I can see in the picture and say what they're doing.

In the foreground, I can see a man standing by a pile of luggage. To the right of him, two men are talking. And to the right of the two men, a young couple are looking at some information on a tablet computer. In the middle of the picture, what seems to be a businessman is running to catch a train. In the background, two people are buying tickets, an elderly man is walking slowly towards the ticket barrier, and two people are taking the escalator up to the train platform.

There is more I could describe, but I hope this gives a clear overall impression of the scene.

Practice 4.1 – Explanation

Response B is the best response. The grammar, vocabulary, and language use are all natural and correct. It uses the same logical organization as Task 3 and discusses the same people in the same order, which is good. It makes reasonable and natural predictions about what the people in the scene might do next. A response like this would probably get a score of 11 to 12.

In contrast, Response A is poorly organized: the speaker jumps around from person to person in the scene and does make predictions in a clear, logical order. This makes it harder for the rater to follow the response. In addition, the language is very repetitive: the speaker uses "might" to introduce each prediction. This kind of repetitive language is likely to reduce the speaker's overall score.

Response C also has problems. It uses a better order than response A, but it is even more repetitive: the speaker uses the phrase "will probably continue" in each prediction. This kind of repetitive language is likely to reduce the speaker's overall score. In addition, the speaker says that every person will continue doing what he or she was already doing, which is not what the raters are listening for because it is not really a prediction.

Practice 4.2 – Completed Response

I'll predict what **some of the people** in this park scene might do next and some of the things that might happen next.

I suspect that the two elderly people will continue cycling **down the street** in the direction they **are currently heading**. I feel that the young couple who are wearing backpacks will let their dog **run around in** the park **in order to** get some exercise. The two women taking a selfie will probably take several pictures before **looking at their phone** to decide which selfie is the best one they took. I feel that the parents of the two children who are playing with a ball will say that lunch is ready and then **the whole family** will probably have a picnic on the grass. Finally, I feel that the hot air balloon will float off to the east.

Obviously **I cannot be sure** any of these predictions will come true, but perhaps some of them will.

Practice 4.3 – Corrected Response

I'll predict what some of the people in this bus station scene might do next and some of the things that might happen next.

I suspect that the people **who are waiting** in the bus shelter will **pick up** their bags and get on a bus that **will take** them to their destination. I feel that the people walking on the road by the bus will either board a bus **or** move onto the sidewalk. At the café, the woman will finish ordering her coffee and then probably sit down and start **to drink** it. I imagine that the people shaking hands will go and get a coffee together so they can chat with each other **more easily**. I think the two men with beards might decide to use their phones **in order to** make a call or perhaps even take **a** photo.

Obviously I cannot be sure any of these predictions will come true, but perhaps some of them will.

Practice 4.4 – Suggested Response

I'll predict what some of the people in this railway station scene might do next and some of the things that might happen next.

I suspect that the man standing by the pile of luggage will meet a friend who will then pick up some of the luggage. I think that the two men will continue their conversation. I imagine that the young couple will buy train tickets after they have finished looking at the tablet. I think the businessman who is running might either trip over or run into somebody. The two people buying tickets and the elderly man will all take the escalator up to the platform. And the people already on the escalator will reach the platform and sit or stand while they wait for their train to arrive.

Obviously I cannot be sure that any of these predictions will come true, but perhaps at least some of them will.

Practice 5.1 – Explanation

Response B is the better response. The grammar, vocabulary, and language use are all natural and correct. It clearly states the speaker's preference for which restaurant to visit and gives two reasons with relevant supporting details and examples. A response like this would probably get a score of 11 to 12.

In contrast, Response A uses accurate and natural grammar and vocabulary, but it does not address the topic. Task 5 questions tell you to persuade the other person why the option you chose is better than the option that he or she chose. In this response, the speaker does not do this. Instead, he argues that the best option is to ask his sister where she would like to go. In real life, this may be the best option, but in a test like CELPIP, not doing what the task asks you to do may significantly reduce your score.

Practice 5.2 – Completed Response

The city you chose definitely has **some good points**. However, there are a couple of reasons why I think my choice is the better option for our visit to the USA.

For one thing, I didn't **tell you this yet**, but my boss has asked me to go to Boston to attend a conference next month. Moreover, **I spent a few days** in Boston several years ago on business. **As I'm sure that** you can understand, I **would rather go** somewhere I've never been before, which is why New York is my preference.

For another thing, a couple of days ago you and I talked about **what we want to do** on our trip. **We both agreed that** going to museums and the theatre would be great. I know that Boston has museums and theatres, too, but New York is **much more famous** for these kinds of cultural attractions.

I hope you understand and agree with my reasons for thinking that we'd have a better time in New York.

Practice 5.3 – Corrected Response

The sofa you **chose** definitely has some good points. However, there are a couple of reasons why I think my choice is the **better** option for our shared home.

First, sometimes we have friends or family members, such as my sister or your brother, come to **stay** at our home, and it would be great to have a sofa bed for a guest **to** sleep on.

Second, **although** I usually like leather sofas, I think the two shades of grey of the Italian-made sofa will look better in our home **than** the brown leather and fabric of your **suggested** sofa.

Finally, I think it would be good to have a sofa with **enough space** for more than two people. My option is the only sofa with room for three people to sit.

I hope you understand and agree with my reasons for feeling that the Italian-made sofa is a better option.

Practice 5.4 – Suggested Response

The hotel you chose definitely has some good points. However, there are a couple of reasons why I think my choice is the better option for my business trip next week.

First, the Silver Star Hotel is much closer to downtown than the Airport Traveller Hotel. This is important because I will be meetings numerous clients downtown. I think it will save me a lot of time if I don't have to travel almost 20 kilometers to and from the hotel.

In addition, the Silver Star Hotel is more modern and looks more attractive. In contrast, the Airport Traveller Hotel looks kind of old-fashioned. I will meet some clients at my hotel, and I think that a modern-looking hotel is likely to make a better impression on them.

I hope you understand and agree with my reasons for thinking that the Silver Star Hotel is a better option.

Practice 6.1 – Explanation

Response B is the better response. The grammar, vocabulary, and language use are all natural and correct. It clearly states which option the speaker has chosen and gives two reasons why. Both reasons are natural, relevant to the topic, and supported with details and examples. A response like this would probably get a score of 11 to 12.

Response A, in contrast, has a number of problems. For one thing, the speaker does not directly say why the first reason means he cannot drive his friend to the job interview. For another thing, the second body section is a suggestion for what his friend could do rather than a reason why he cannot drive the friend to the interview. It is OK to include suggestions in your response, but it is better to give a reason first, and then a suggestion.

Practice 6.2 – Completed Response

Hi, Mom and Dad. **I hope you're well**. Many thanks for the invitation to come round for a family dinner on Sunday. **I've decided** that I'm not going to come because I'm going to have dinner with my friend Maria instead. There are **a couple of reasons** for my decision.

First, Maria is going away on a long business trip soon, and this will be **my last chance** to see her for about six months. I want to **have an opportunity** to chat with her before she goes away. I'm sure that **you can understand**.

Second, we had a family dinner just a couple of weeks ago, and Thanksgiving is coming up soon, so I think we'll have plenty more opportunities to **spend time together** in the near future.

This was not **an easy choice** for me, but I'm sure you can understand and respect my reasons for choosing to have dinner with Maria on Sunday rather than with you.

Practice 6.3 – Corrected Response

Hi, Michael. I've been thinking about whether to **go to** Hawaii with you or with Brian. I'm sorry to say that **I've decided** to go with my brother. There are a couple of reasons for my **choice**.

First, my brother has had a hard time recently. His wife left him, he **was** sick, and then he lost his job. Going to Hawaii with you would be great, but I think **that** Brian deserves a chance to relax and enjoy himself more.

Second, last time you and **I** spoke, you seemed worried about your work situation. I remember you saying that you **have been** working really hard because of concern that you might lose your job. I am worried that if you take time off now, your boss might decide you are not serious about your job.

This was not an easy choice for me, but I **hope** you understand my reasons for choosing to go with Brian.

Test Expert Speaking Practice *for* **CELPIP**®

Practice 6.4 – Suggested Response

Hi, Jenny. I understand your feelings about continuing to pay part of Dan's rent every month, but I'm sorry to say that I'm going to carry on paying. There are a couple of reasons why.

First, if we both stop paying, Dan will not be able to pay his rent. I'm worried he might lose his apartment as a result. If that happens, he would have to move in with you or me, but neither of us has a large home.

Second, I agree that Dan's old enough to solve his own problems, but I don't think we can just stop financial help without warning. I think we should tell him of our plan and give him three months to get a better job before we stop helping him.

This was not an easy choice for me, but I hope you can understand and accept my reasons.

Practice 7.1 – Explanation

Response A is the better response. The grammar, vocabulary, and language use are all natural and correct. It clearly states a position on the issue and gives two reasons with details and supporting examples. A response like this would probably get a score of 11 to 12.

Response B, in contrast, has a number of problems. For one thing, it is somewhat short and the speaker would probably finish saying it rather early. For another thing, although the phrase "make money and be productive members of society" is natural, correct English, the speaker repeats it too often. Finally, the reasons are not supported with details or examples.

Practice 7.2 – Completed Response

I can see why some people might disagree with banning advertisements for unhealthy foods like candy or potato chips. From my **point of view**, however, there are several reasons why doing this would **be a good idea**.

First and foremost, more and more young people are suffering from health issues these days. These health issues include diabetes and being overweight. From what I have read and heard, unhealthy food is **a major cause** of these problems, and I think that banning ads for such food would mean people purchase and eat bad food less often, which might improve the situation.

And second, I think that if companies were only allowed to advertise healthy foods, they would soon change their policies. Currently, many companies produce unhealthy food items, but under the new law, I think they would start developing and advertising healthier foods. These ads **may persuade people** to begin eating these foods, and this would definitely improve people's health, **in my view**.

To sum up, for **the reasons given**, I think ads for unhealthy foods should definitely be banned. I hope the government decides to do this as **soon as possible**.

Practice 7.3 – Corrected Response

This is a difficult question for me to answer because I can see both sides of **this issue**.

On the one hand, if children were required to do physical exercise **every day** at school, I am sure they would be much fitter and healthier. This would be beneficial because they would be sick less often, which would mean their parents wouldn't have to stay **at** home to look **after** them because they must be absent from school.

On the other hand, the purpose of school is to educate children. I think teachers should spend their time helping children **to learn** how to read, how to write, how to calculate, how to solve problems, and so on. If schoolchildren have to spend part of each day running around or doing some kind of sport, obviously they will have **less** time for serious learning.

In conclusion, it is hard to answer this question, but on the whole I think that requiring students to play sports or do some **other** kind of physical activity is a good idea. I hope that schools in my **neighbourhood** start doing this as soon as possible.

Practice 7.4 – Suggested Response

I can see why some people might think having one public holiday a month would be too many. In my view, however, there are several reasons why doing this would be a good idea.

For one thing, these days, most people have very busy, stressful lives. For example, I work six days a week, and on my day off I have to clean my home, buy groceries, and so on. Public holidays are one of the only days when I can relax and do what I want, so I am definitely in favour of having more of them.

For another thing, because people are so busy, they often find it hard to spend quality time with friends or family members. My wife also works six days a week, but her day off is not the same as mine. As a result, we rarely get to spend time together. We both get public holidays off, however, and could do more things together if such holidays were more frequent.

To sum up, for the reasons mentioned, I support the idea of Canada having one public holiday each month. I hope the government decides to do this.

Practice 8.1 – Explanation

Response C is the best response. The grammar, vocabulary, and language use are all natural and correct. The response is logically organized in that the speaker describes the general features of the painting first and then moves on to talk about specific details. The response gives a clear description of the painting and addresses every part of the task well. A response like this would probably get a score of 11 to 12.

In contrast, Response A has some problems. In terms of content, the speaker does not say that the image is made up of small and large dots, which is probably the main feature of the painting. This will affect the speaker's score. In terms of organization, the response jumps around and is not well organized. The speaker talks about one hand, then mentions jumping, then talks about the other hand, and so on. And in terms of language use, the speaker uses unnatural repetition by saying "the painting" rather than "it" and "he or she" rather than just "he" or just "she."

Test Expert Speaking Practice *for* **CELPIP**®

Response B also has a number of problems. For one thing, the speaker does not make it clear that the guitarist in the picture is made of dots. This means his description is not as clear as it could be. In addition, the speaker gives his opinion about what is happening in the painting by saying "he's probably ... playing at a concert." In Task 8 questions, it is better to describe what you see than to imagine what you cannot see. Finally, the speaker wastes time describing things like the frame of the picture that are not major features.

Practice 8.2 – Completed Response

Hi. I'm calling because I think there's **a chance that** by mistake you left your keys **at my place**. I'll describe them for you.

There's a ring in the middle which has **a number of** keys and objects attached to it. One key is a car key. It has a black part with a picture of a car on it **as well as** buttons to lock and unlock the car doors. Next to that is **what looks to be** some USB memory. It has the number "32" and the letters "GB" on it **at the bottom**. Next to that is what seems to be a pocket for holding credit cards **or perhaps** a driver's licence. Finally, there are two keys that are linked together. One looks like it is made of metal. The other **appears to have** a square plastic top.

I hope my description of the keys is clear. Do you think they're yours?

Practice 8.3 – Corrected Response

Hi. I'm calling because I saw an image that might be a great logo for your business. **Let me** describe it for you.

The image **shows** a tree. The main part of the tree and the branches are black and **look like** a normal tree. The leaves of the tree are interesting and different, **however**. For one thing, the image has different kinds of fruit **rather than** real leaves. These fruits include strawberries, pineapples, grapes, apples, melons, cherries, oranges, **and** other varieties. In addition, the fruits suggest good **health** because they are in the shape of a heart.

I hope my description of the image is clear. Do you think that it **might** be a good logo for your fruit store?

Practice 8.4 – Suggested Response

Hello. I'm calling because my sister sent me a picture of some cakes from your bakery that I want to know about. Let me describe them for you.

One cake is in the shape of a cube. It looks like it has two layers with cream in the middle. It also appears to have cream and a strawberry on top. Another cake is in the shape of a triangle. It's made of many thin layers. On top it looks like it has three chocolate balls and some melted chocolate. The final one is a round cake. I'm not sure if this is the correct word, but it looks like it's in a paper cup. It has some small bits on top as well as a cookie or something in the top.

I hope my description of the cakes is clear. Do you happen to know the names of the cakes that I described?

APPENDIX 1 – OTHER STUDY MATERIALS

After you have reviewed and practiced all of the speaking questions, practice exercises, and challenges in this book, you may want to find other study materials that you can use to continue practicing. Here are some suggestions:

1. Create your own topics for Tasks 1, 2, 6, and 7 by making small changes to the topics in this book

It is relatively easy to come up with new topics by adapting the topics in this book (or other books). For example, you could change Practice 1.1 on page 18 from

> **A family member is deciding where to go on vacation. She will either go somewhere in Canada or somewhere in the United States. Give her some advice about where to go.**

to

> **A <u>friend</u> is deciding where to go on <u>a family</u> vacation. <u>He and his family</u> will either go somewhere in <u>Europe</u> or somewhere in <u>Asia</u>. Give <u>him</u> some advice about where to go.**

Small changes like this are easy to make and give you the opportunity to get a lot of extra practice for free.

2. Create your own topics for Tasks 3, 4, and 8 by finding new pictures on the Internet

It is easy to search the Internet for pictures. Google has a useful image search, and most stock image websites will also let you search their database of images for free.

To find useful pictures for Tasks 3 and 4, try searching for images of "people in a shopping mall" or "people on a beach" or "people in a meeting" or similar. (Note that even though the pictures in CELPIP tend to be drawings, not photographs, describing what you can see in a photograph (or predicting what might happen next) would still give you valuable speaking practice.

To find useful pictures for Task 8, search for something like "unusual animal" or "strange costume" or "weird object." Again, even though the questions in CELPIP show you drawings rather than photographs, describing photographs of unusual things would definitely give you useful practice.

3. Create your own topics for Task 5 by finding pictures on the Internet and making up your own details

Search for images of three similar things, such as tablet computers, refrigerators, holiday resorts, and so on. Come up with three to five pieces of similar information – such as price, size, location, and so on – about each thing. Then practice coming up with a response based on the pictures and information you made up.

4. Adapt speaking questions from other tests

Most English tests, such as IELTS or TOEFL, have a speaking section. Some of the speaking questions in these tests are similar to the speaking tasks in CELPIP. There are many good study books for IELTS, TOEFL, and TOEIC Speaking and Writing that have questions that may be useful for CELPIP. You should be able to buy these (or borrow them from a library, if you prefer).

These tests and questions include:

- Speaking Task 2 questions in TOEFL iBT are similar to CELPIP Speaking Task 1 questions
- Speaking Task 1 questions in TOEFL iBT are similar to CELPIP Speaking Task 2 questions
- Speaking Task 3 questions in TOEIC Speaking and Writing are similar to CELPIP Speaking Task 3 questions
- Speaking Task 3 questions in TOEIC Speaking and Writing can also be used for CELPIP Speaking Task 4
- Speaking Task 1 and Task 2 questions in TOEFL iBT are similar to CELPIP Speaking Task 7 questions

(Note that there are no speaking tasks in other tests that are similar to CELPIP Speaking Tasks 5, 6, or 8. For these tasks, you should use some of the other suggestions to find additional practice questions.)

5. Borrow or purchase official CELPIP study materials

Paragon Testing Enterprises is the organization that develops and administers the CELPIP Test. This organization sells official practice tests and study materials for CELPIP. Some of these materials focus only on speaking; other materials cover every part of the CELPIP test.

You may be able to borrow these from a local library. If this is not possible, you may be able to purchase them online from Amazon.ca or from this website: https://www.paragontesting.ca/

6. Find unofficial CELPIP speaking questions on the Internet

You can also find unofficial speaking questions for CELPIP if you search the Internet. You should be careful with unofficial topics that you find, however. Unlike the topics you see in official CELPIP study materials or the questions in this book, which have been carefully designed to closely resemble official questions, some unofficial questions that you find online may not be similar to the official test. If you worry that a question you found online is not a good question, it may be better not to use that question.

APPENDIX 2 – PICTURES

Task 3, pages 32–37
Task 4, pages 44–49

Task 3, page 38
Task 4, page 50

Test Expert Speaking Practice *for* **CELPIP**®

Task 3, page 40
Task 4, page 52

Task 3, page 41
Task 4, page 53

Task 3, page 42
Task 4, page 54

Task 3, page 43
Task 4, page 55

Test Expert Speaking Practice *for* **CELPIP**®

Task 8, pages 94–99

Task 8, page 100

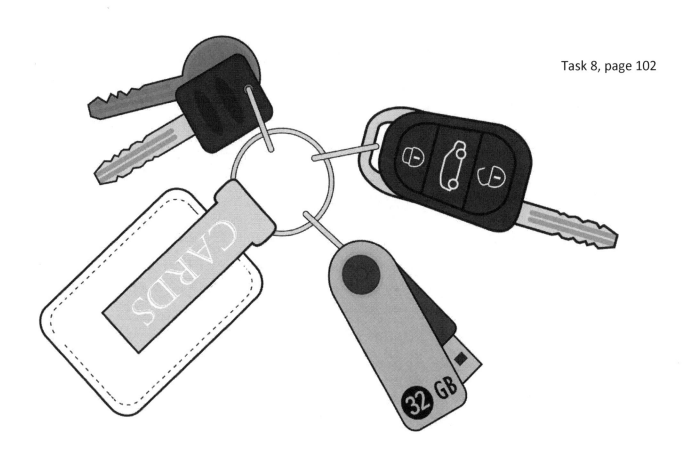

Test Expert Speaking Practice *for* **CELPIP**®

Task 8, page 104

Task 8, page 105

NOTES

Manufactured by Amazon.ca
Bolton, ON

11233884R00070